Seven Angels for Seven Days

Seven ANGELS FOR Seven DAYS
Angelina Fast-Vlaar

CASTLE QUAY BOOKS

Published by:
Castle Quay Books
500 Trillium Drive, Kitchener, Ontario, N2G 4Y4
Tel: (800) 265-6397   Fax (519) 748-9835

Copy editing by Janet Dimond
Cover Design by John Cowie, *eyetoeye design*
Printed at Essence Publishing, Belleville, Ontario

Dedicated to my dear children:
David, James, Ruth Anne, Bruce and Wayne.
In loving memory of
Peter.

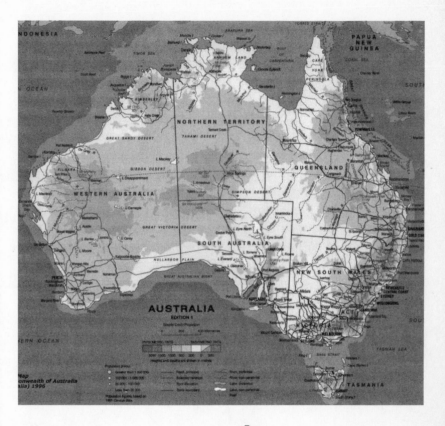

Australia

Contents

Acknowledgements

First of all, my thanks goes to our Lord, the "Shepherd and Overseer" of our souls. I thank Him for His hand in the events of this story and in the telling of it.

When discouragement set in during chemotherapy treatments in 1998, I turned to the Scriptures for comfort and came upon "I will not die but live, and will proclaim what the Lord has done" (Psalm 118:17).

I sensed a three-fold message. First, I would survive the cancer. Second, I was to arrange the journal I had been keeping into a book. This became *The Valley of Cancer: A Journey of Comfort and Hope* (1999, 2003, Essence Publishing).

And third, I sensed a deeper, somewhat familiar nudging. There was another story tucked away in my 1987–1989 journals, and now was the time to bring it to light and share "what the Lord has done."

Thank you to the many who, in one way or another, became part of this story.

Thank you Steve, Michelle, Margaret, Doug, Loretta, Marge, Merv and Graham, for your part in the tale. I'll never forget it.

It was difficult to go back and relive this earlier experience, and the writing progressed at a snail's pace. Thank you, Inscribe Christian Fellowship, for awarding the first chapter a prize in 2001. It spurred me on.

Thank you, Ray Wiseman, for your positive critique in 2003 and for impressing upon me the importance of completing the work.

My children received a copy as a Christmas gift in 2003. Thank you, kids, for your encouragement to share this slice of our lives with others.

Thank you, Suzanne Harssema, for asking to read the manuscript. You turned out to be the editor I needed at that point and your excitement was so contagious!

Thank you, Donna Mann, for your friendship, your prayers, and your sensitive "reader's ear." You give so freely.

And Janet Dimond—I was so thankful the "angels" landed in your kind, capable hands. Thank you for your editorial skill as you polished their wings for takeoff!

A special thank you to Larry Willard, my publisher, and Gus Henne of Essence, who chose me for the "Best New Canadian Christian Author" award. Thank you, Larry, for being gentle with my "heart." Thank you for your guidance and expertise—for getting "all the stars in place!"

Thank you, The Word Guild, for creating opportunities for writers who dream.

Thank you, Castle Quay Books and Essence Publishing, for making dreams come true!

And to you, Joe. Thank you for your love, support, and patient understanding. Thank you for cheering me on to the finish! I love you.

Prologue

It all begins when the telephone rings on a lovely spring day in May of '87. Peter lifts the receiver, and immediately I know it's the expected call from our son Jim in Australia.

"A boy?"

"Congratulations!"

"Dylan James! Very nice!"

"Julie and baby fine?"

After a few more exchanges, he replaces the receiver, turns to me, face beaming, and with the familiar glint of humour in his eyes says, "Imagine! We receive a phone call on May 14th to tell us our grandson was born on May 15th!" Then, staring out the window, eyes now misty, he softly adds, "I *must* go to Australia to see my new grandson."

Throughout May and June, Peter patiently tries to persuade me to take a trip down under. A long trip—at least six months. He's retired from his teaching career with an early pension so is free to go. He feels I can "easily" take two terms off from my part-time teaching position, and the trip can be our thirtieth wedding anniversary celebration.

One day he comes home, fetches our big atlas, opens it to a map of Australia, and plunks the book on the dining room table.

"There!" he says, his eyes holding mine as if to say, "That's where we're going!"

e atlas remains on the table, open, and now and then Peter
ne about the fascinating island continent. It brings back memories of him telling the same stories nearly thirty years ago when he
taught his grade eights a course about Australia. I know it's a dream
of his to go and see the beauty for himself.

One day he bursts into the house with one of his "Guess what!"
exclamations. His sister and brother-in-law have booked a trip to
Australia! He marches to the dining room table, points to the atlas and
says, "We can have a grand family reunion with my niece, Loretta, in
Adelaide." With his finger on the map he adds, "We can drive through
the outback to get there!" I merely glance as his finger traces the route.

"What's stopping us?" he asks.

His health is stopping me—heart surgery eighteen years ago,
more surgery recommended six years ago but cancelled due to a
poor prognosis. A daily regimen of drugs helps to keep the choles-
terol levels low and the angina pain manageable.

One afternoon in late June, I settle in one of the blue rockers by
the bay window overlooking our wooded backyard, knowing that,
eventually, I'll have to reach a conclusion about whether or not to
embark on such a long journey.

I pick up my Bible and read Psalm 139. The ninth and tenth
verses jump out: "If I rise on the wings of the dawn, if I settle on the
far side of the sea, even there your hand will guide me, your right
hand will hold me fast."

It catches my breath. It may just as well read, "If you fly all the
way to Australia on the other side of the ocean and settle there for a
time, I will look after you completely." Words of reassurance: God
watches over us no matter where we are.

The front door opens, and in a moment, Peter stands in the living room. He has a way of filling a room just by entering it. He fas-
tens his eyes on me and I know something important is about to be
said. In a determined, almost aggressive tone, he states: "I *am* going
to Australia. The only thing that will stop me is my dead body."

His eyes hold mine as he waits for the words to sink in. His
breath comes short and fast. Behind his grey beard and moustache

I can see his mouth drawn tight. I know he is expecting my usual resistance and he seems ready to challenge it. I also wait a moment, for effect, and then softly say, "It's all right, Hon; we'll go."

He stands motionless, staring. Then his face opens up and I watch the rapidly changing emotions wash over it: disbelief, wonder, surprise, pleasure. His blue eyes find their sparkle again; his mouth curves into his generous smile. He slowly crosses the room and bends down to kiss me. I show him the Scripture and start to read, but my voice breaks. He nods and smiles.

"Six months?" he softly says.

"Sure. I'll call the college tomorrow."

With the decision made, the scenery changes. We excitedly prepare for our trip of a lifetime. The children cheer us on and Peter takes ample time to say goodbye to family, friends and neighbours.

We fly out on September 12th, and, crossing the International Date Line, we miss the 13th, our anniversary! We spend five beautiful weeks with Jim and Julie in Palm Cove, an idyllic coastal town just north of Cairns. Besides doting on Dylan, we take long walks, relax on the beach, play in the ocean, read in the shade of the palms, savour tea at the Tea House, and explore some of the surrounding sights. We plan a six-week camping trip to Adelaide and intend to be back in Palm Cove to celebrate Christmas together with the children.

We buy a car and Peter suggests we take it for a test drive to Cape Tribulation. We drive north from Palm Cove, and after several hours come to the Daintree River crossing.

Part I

Journey into the Desert

1987

*Remember how the LORD your God led
you all the way in the desert...in order
to know what was in your heart
(Deuteronomy 8:2).*

1

Cape Tribulation

Saturday, October 10, 1987

The swollen river looks menacing, threatening. The ferry, a low-lying barge, inches across the wide iron-coloured expanse of water.

Peter wanders over to the captain. He asks about us and Peter informs him that we're from Canada.

"Heard about this year's croc attacks, Mate?" the man asks.

"We've heard some," Peter answers.

"A tourist was one victim," the captain says, holding Peter's eye in a piercing gaze. "Stupid tourists!" The man continues, "Can't they just read our signs? Obey them?"

I remember seeing the crocodile warning signs as we drove up the rickety ramp onto the boat.

The captain now stares in the Daintree, shakes his head and, lowering his voice, says, "Lady from here, two years ago. Tossed in the air—gone. No sound; no blood."

"We heard," Peter says softly.

I shudder and shuffle to the centre of the ferry. I glance at the black water. What lurks beneath the surface? The jaws of death?

The captain looks us over, eyes our car.

"Where are you going?" he asks.

"To the cape," Peter answers, mustering confidence.

"The cape?" he asks incredulously. He holds Peter's eye and continues, "You'll be needing a four-wheel drive, Mate!"

Peter shrugs and grins.

"That's what Jim said," I whisper.

Captain Cook gave the cape its ominous name and I wonder...

I glance at the car we bought last week for $600. A light-grey 1967 Toyota Corona. Peter was delighted with our find and promptly dubbed her Bessie. Now the car looks small and pale and weak parked behind two sturdy steel-boned open vehicles. Like a sickly child with two strong parents.

We roll off the ferry and follow the track into the forest—a track barely wide enough for one vehicle. Large potholes, sharp rocks and tree roots make up its surface. The car lunges from side to side.

A creek appears. There is no bridge in sight.

"I guess we have to drive through it," Peter quips.

Another vehicle drives up and proceeds straight into the water a few metres downstream. "This is what you do, Mate," laughs the female driver leaning out the window, water splashing.

This needs a photo. I hop out of the car, kick off my shoes, wade into the creek on smooth pebbles and wait for Bessie to "swim" across. She stalls in the middle of the creek. She starts but stalls again and again, water spurting out of her tailpipe. Finally—the motor turns over once more and she haltingly makes it through the water and up the low bank on the other side.

I'm still standing in the water when I see the sign—bold black letters painted on a white board—"Warning! Crocodiles. Do not go in the water!"

I glance about, heart pounding. Where? That log? Peter has also spotted the sign and yells, "What are you *doing*? Get *out* of that water!"

I lift my feet high like a long-legged bird so as not to create a splash and hurry across, run to the car and slam the door shut. *Stupid tourist.*

"You OK?" Peter asks.

"I'm all right."

We drive further into the forest.

Suddenly we jolt to a stop and I lunge forward, barely missing the windshield.

Peter decides the brakes must have locked because of the water. We can't budge Bessie, no matter what we try. She's planted her wheels firmly on the ground like a stubborn mule.

"Someone will come along eventually," Peter says softly, leaning against the car.

We're all alone. The jungle suddenly seems awfully still and creepy. We're secluded in a world apart, hidden within the massive trees and no one knows we're here.

Birds caw and chirp, trill and whistle, now here, then there, as if to pass the word along that visitors (*stupid tourists)* have arrived. And how long will these be stranded here?

Finally—we hear a rumbling sound and for a moment I fear it's a large animal lumbering through the trees toward us. After several minutes, a jeep bumps up with three noisy, friendly young men who reassure us with the typical, "No worries, Mate." However, they also can't budge Bessie.

"There's a mechanic three kilometres back," they tell us. "You can catch a ride with the bus. It should be along shortly."

A bus?

A noisy open vehicle appears that looks like an old rusty army truck with the top down. I climb in; Peter stays with the car.

"The mechanic lives on top of that hill," the bus driver tells me as we emerge from the forest.

I climb the long hill and find the mechanic. He grabs some tools and says, "All right, let's go."

I climb into his truck and he starts out but then stops because another vehicle is climbing the hill, backwards! I recognize Bessie.

Peter jumps out and laughs, "She wouldn't go forward, so I drove her backwards!" His eyes crackle with daring and mischief.

"You drove in reverse all that way through the creek and along that awful track?"

"Yep," he answers, a triumphant grin spread all over his face.

The mechanic fixes our problem and suggests we not go through any more creeks–there are three more to cross before we get to the cape! He advises us to camp at Crocodylus Village, a backpackers' hideaway in the forest. A canvas and pole structure, set several feet off the forest floor, is available to us. Peter is delighted to sleep in a "tree house"!

After supper I go for a walk on one of the pebble paths that crinkle through the enchanting forest. Enchanting until...another sign. "Warning! Crocodiles. Do not leave the path!" I turn on my heels, run back to our tent, clamber up the ladder, slam the door. *Stupid...*

"What's the matter?" Peter asks, looking up from his book.

"Another sign. Crocodiles," I gasp.

"What? You saw one?"

"No, a sign."

"Well, stay in here then," he says. "Come, sit down, listen to this. Paton wrote this book while his wife was dying..." (*Instrument of Thy Peace*). I listen with one ear, the other cocked to the night sounds of the forest.

When it's bedtime, I check the door, the windows.

"Nothing will climb up, right? No snakes, no crocs...?"

"Don't worry, we'll be fine."

"You always say that."

Sunday, October 11

Peter is noticeably restless. Finally he blurts out, "We aren't going to let a few creeks beat us, are we? Let's go to the cape."

"And get stuck again?"

"The water will be lower in the creeks because the tide is still low. Let's hurry."

Despite my misgivings, we set out, navigate the narrow bumpy track, and cross all four creeks.

We make it to the cape! It's nothing more than a small clearing, a shack, a few tents, a rounded patch of powdery beach, yet it's so much more. Dense green forest hems us in on three sides. The Coral

Sea stretches out before us; it sparkles like blue crystal. Unbelievable peace and stillness envelope us. All that reaches our ears is the music of the birds and the measured breathing of the water—long soft sighs released on the sandy shore. It seems like the very end of civilization. It truly is the end of the road.

"This was well worth it," Peter sighs.

After a long while he whispers, "We *have* to go. The water is rising."

With another sigh, we drive back into the forest and successfully cross the creeks.

Peter believes the car has stood the test despite some needed repairs, and we can now safely drive into the outback. I'm not convinced. On the third morning of our camping trip...

2

Crossroads

Steel thunder explodes around our tent, jolts us awake. Shocked and bewildered, it takes us a moment to find a label for the din. Peter is the first to mumble, "Train." The monster tears the morning stillness with what sounds like a reverberating scream. The bed, on which a moment ago we slept so soundly, vibrates—the train's wheels so close I fear they might suck us in, carrying us along in their hurtling speed. I shield my ears from the assault and wait, heart pounding, for the rolling racket to pass, the wailing to fade—wait for the silence to mend. I glance at my watch; it's 6 o'clock.

Wide awake now, Peter turns and hoarsely whispers, "Let's go."

We slip into our shorts and T-shirts and emerge from the camper trailer into the soft light of an Australian dawn. I walk to the wire fence against which we set up camp last night at dusk, and peer over a mass of tropical plants. A railway embankment runs along the entire back length of the campground! We chose this secluded spot for privacy and quiet and wondered why the other campers had avoided all the great sites along the fence!

We pack in silence, not wanting to disturb the morning stillness again, as most of the other campers seem to have slept through the roar of the train. Also, because just now there is not much to say.

We've said it all. We've come to a crossroads here in Townsville, and we still disagree on which road to take. Peter wants to drive through the outback to reach Adelaide; I want to continue south along the east coast. I'm uneasy about travelling through the outback—the land they call *Never-Never*. The term alone frightens me, as in: *you'll never, never make it.* I'd feel safer driving along the ocean, maybe as far as Sydney, and this way skirt most of the desert. But the outback lures Peter.

Packing our gear is a bit of a challenge. We're borrowing Jim's camper trailer for our six-week *walkabout*. The camper's large extended tent needs to be properly folded to make it fit on top of the camper bed, and it's difficult to do so without communicating. The silence hangs between us like a gossamer veil.

I notice the sky glowing orange behind the tall trees that surround the campground and a sudden sadness catches my throat. Our holiday has been so beautiful, but this morning is different. It's marked with discord: a train's ominous roar, tension between us, and we're missing the sunrise—the sun slowly lifting her amber self out of the ocean, dripping golden droplets as it were, and casting her first oblique light.

We finally finish packing and I take the last armful of stuff to the car. I notice two four-gallon containers of water standing on the floor. Peter must have bought them yesterday when grocery shopping. I stare at them…s*urely he won't venture…*

We slide into the car and Peter slowly drives past the wiser campers, past the pool, past the office, toward the gate. He stops and I hold my breath. His strong, broad hands are at the top of the steering wheel and slowly, deliberately, hand over hand, he turns the wheel and the car curves west onto the Flinder's Highway, which will lead us straight into the land that lies *behind the back of beyond.* He's made the decision—we're going to go through the desert.

Peter's stubborn way of sticking to his point of view has often been a source of strain in our relationship, but I sense there is something else going on here. He seems to need to take this desert route for some reason—maybe to fulfill a long-held cherished dream. Whatever it is, I'm going along. We're in this together. I steal a glance, but his eyes are on the quiet street as we drive through town. When the road opens up, he turns his head and grins. His blue eyes glint certain mischief. I shake my head and avert my eyes, but gradually I sense a warmth creep around my heart and I return the smile. I love this man, this handsome, grey-bearded, fun-loving man. I love him for his strength, his zest for life, his sense of self, despite the frustration it sometimes brings. I feel a twinge of excitement now about the trip ahead. If he feels confident to do it, I'm also game to take this journey into the outback. I just didn't want to be the one to make the decision, the one to be responsible.

The tension dissipates. The curtain lifts.

Out of Townsville, the highway cuts through a forested area. Trees line the road and seem to embrace us protectively; at times, the branches form a canopy over us.

"This isn't so bad; look at all the trees!" I exclaim. "I hope they'll stay with us for awhile."

"We're not far from the coast during this first stretch."

"I'd like to be eased into the outback scene gradually," I remark.

"We'll be just fine."

"You always say that."

"And haven't I also always been right?"

"Yes, Hon, you're right." I say it kindly.

The highway turns west. The trees become sparse and stunted, revealing more and more of the dry, dusty red soil. I glance at Peter. He's concentrating, trying to miss the largest of the potholes in the road. The car jounces and swerves from side to side.

"If the road is this bad close to town, what will it be like when there are no towns?" I ask.

"We'll be fine. People travel here, you know."

Travel? Only one vehicle has rumbled by!

I stare at the lonely landscape as it flits past the car window and wonder what lies ahead.

"It's starting to look more like the outback, I suppose," Peter remarks.

"Yes, look at the colour of the soil! They say the outback sand is red, but here it looks more like curry powder, don't you think?"

"Hmm."

"Like coriander over there where the sun glimpses through the trees. And there's a bit of nutmeg under those shrubs."

"Yeah, I guess, if you have to be so descriptive." Peter turns and grins affectionately.

Beige-coloured cows stand forlorn here and there among the scrubby trees. They stare at us with sad, doleful eyes. Their punched-out skeletons tell of scarcity of food and drink. Red, pitted anthills, several metres tall, stand like rusty grave monuments among the thirsty trees. They're actually termite mounds and look impressively alike with their ridged turrets, as if the insect architects had one blueprint.

The road stretches out before us; the sun climbs overhead; the temperature rises.

3

Never-Never Land

A small town slowly materializes ahead of us. Charters Towers. We drive onto the wide main street. A white-pillared building glistens in the sun. Lower, darker buildings line the street.

"Where are the people?" I whisper.

"Remember, the guide book says the people left when the mine closed."

"Looks like a ghost town."

We walk a bit, feel rather lost in this deserted, eerie space. We spot a café and walk toward it to buy a cup of coffee.

Suddenly, a piercing, agonizing wail. Stunned, we turn around.

An Aborigine woman staggers up the street.

"I'm just a dirty nigger; I'm just a dirty nigger," she howls over and over.

I cringe to hear her cry the demeaning words. She moves closer, swaying, blubbering out her pain. She flops to the ground, sprawled out, her skirt around her waist, her nakedness exposed.

Shaken, I glance around. The street is virtually empty.

"You go help her," Peter whispers.

I approach the woman, bend down, and pull her skirt back over her bare legs.

"How can I help you?" I ask softly.

"I'm thirsty," she croaks.

"I'll get you something. Come, let me help you up."

A thin black hand reaches up. I grasp it and help her to her feet.

"Come and sit down," I say, spotting a chair on the sidewalk in front of the café.

She sits down, still whimpering. I enter the dimly lit building and find a waiter behind a counter.

"There's a lady outside who needs a drink."

"She has to pay."

"I'll look after it. Would you make her a milkshake?"

"What size?"

"Large."

"What flavour?"

"Vanilla."

He hands me a tall paper cup and I go out to give it to the woman.

She reaches for it eagerly, gulps it down, muffles a thank you and shuffles away.

"Good for you," Peter says, hand on my shoulder.

Tears well up. What happened to cause her such distress?

"Let's go in and have a coffee," he suggests.

It's a rather tasteless brew for one reason or another. The Aussies are tea drinkers. The tea is always delicious. *Cooking tea* means to cook the evening meal. I'm still shaken, thinking about the plight of some of the Aborigine people.

"This was such a different encounter than the one on the way to the cape," I finally say.

"Yes, there's another side." Peter smiles encouragingly.

We had stopped for a snack of crackers and jam at a roadside picnic table on our way to Cape Tribulation last week. An Aborigine woman sat at the other end of the table and eyed us curiously. Peter offered her a cracker smeared with jam and she took it eagerly. He offered her another and another. She took each one, giggled with each new offering. It became a game of sorts. Peter said, "She may as well have it all." He scooted the package of crackers, the jar of jam, and the knife her way. She caught all three and laughingly now topped more crackers with jam.

Peter started a conversation and within a few minutes she exclaimed, "You know Jesus? Then you're my brother!"

"Yes, I am!" Peter replied and got up and gave her a bear hug from behind while I ran to the car to fetch the camera.

It's a lovely picture.

Out of Charters Towers the road improves but is reduced to one lane. We pass the very few cars we meet, each with two wheels on the red sand shoulder. A gritty "G'day, Mate" penetrates the dust.

The sun is relentless. Hot air wafts into the car.

"Wouldn't it be cooler with the windows rolled up?"

"Try it."

Now it's stifling hot. I roll them down again, but there is an awful stench.

"What was that?"

"I don't know."

Another whiff of the revolting odour.

"Did you see that?" Peter asks.

"No, what was it?"

"A kangaroo."

"Dead?"

"Yes."

Now I see one and hold my nose. The creature lies at the side of the road, bloated, its beautiful red-brown coat shiny in the sun. We understand the necessity of the *roo-bars* we've seen attached to the front of vehicles.

I count ten decomposing animals in a one-mile stretch.

Trying to shut out the smell of death, I focus on the landscape. Someone could sew a quilt of the scene! A shiny black ribbon stitched on paprika velvet. The velvet edged with mottled rust and green homespun. An outback tapestry!

Noon

We pass through Pentland—a store, school, gas station, hotel, several houses—a cluster of buildings shrouded in dust, silent in the hot hush of noon. Peter eases the car to a stop.

"We could sit in the shade and make a sandwich." Soft-spoken words.

He fishes our little whisk broom from under the driver's seat and sweeps the short length of curb where the skinny tree casts a small patch of shade.

We rummage in our food box; Peter opens a can of sardines, lets the oil dribble on the sand; we make a sandwich.

Every rooftop, every scrawny shrub, every thirsty leaf is covered with a soft layer of dust. Someone has dusted the entire town with dirty pink powder. There is no movement, no sound. How do they cope, this small group of people living here in this heated wilderness?

Suddenly we hear a tiny sound, a happy high-pitched note.

"What was that?"

We strain to hear it again; we're anxious to hear it again.

"It's a child, a child's voice!" Peter says happily.

We don't see anyone, but this bubble of joy streaks across the drab scene like a shooting star on a dark night. It's louder now. At the far end of the street a young man with a little barefoot boy in tow have just turned a corner and are walking toward us. They stop to greet us with the usual friendly "G'day." The man is cheerful and probably not bothered by the heat at all.

"Are you needing the *loo*?" he asks. "It's right over there."

He points to the empty plot across the road, bearded with tufts of yellow grass. Among the grass, rather forlorn, sits a small cement-block building. I walk over to investigate and find two doors and behind them a toilet and a shower!

"Hon, there's a shower!"

This is how they manage: showers! Out for a walk to the store, and they duck in here for a quick cool off. These people need showers. This town needs showers, torrential showers to rinse away the everlasting dust and let some colour shine!

We drive on and stop at a rocky lookout, all of 550 metres high, in the hills of the Great Dividing Range. The now more barren plains stretch away from us in all directions, domed by an enormous sky with a blazing sun. The outback—three million square kilometres. *Forever* is a geographical term here. The immensity of this boundless red earth baffles us, silences us. We're nothing more than two tiny specks in this vast emptiness. I comprehend why they dub it *Never-Never*. Some say the term was coined because those who inhabit it never, never want to leave its stark, bewitching beauty. Jim laughed and said others say the opposite. Those who have lived in the outback and have moved away swear they'll never, never return to it!

Never-Never. Weighted words. It's as if I see them stretched across the horizon, quivering above this sun-scorched land and a shiver of fear runs up my spine.

3 p.m.

We approach Hughenden and see a rectangular building that looks like a forgotten toy block in a mammoth sandbox. It's a motel, complete with camping space and a pool.

"Let's call it a day," Peter says as he swings the car into the grounds.

When he inquires where to set up our camper, the owner stretches his arm in a wide arc-like wave and answers, "Anywhere, Mate."

The tires crunch on red stone that looks like crushed clay pots. Peter stops the car beside one lone pole at the far end of the gravelled space.

"This will do, I guess," he mumbles. Beyond the yard lies the endless stretch of country, speckled with low, dull shrubs. Trees have all but disappeared. Spiky spheres of spinifex grass the size of basketballs nod lazily in the slight breeze. It's difficult to believe cattle eat and thrive on this greyish harsh-looking so-called grass. The withered globe-like plants, broken off from their roots, roll end-over-end like tumbleweeds across the red earth. I watch them roll and then suddenly stop, only to start their rolling tumbles again with the next breath of breeze. They look like children skipping across the plain, playing a game of Mother May I.

We set up camp, change into our *bathers,* and head for the pool. The water brightens our mood.

"I'll get supper started," Peter announces and climbs out.

Floating on my back, weightless, suspended between blue ceramic tile and a deep-blue sky above, my muscles relax, and I wish my soul would do the same. The deep stillness is almost unsettling—the only noise being a thin stream of water splattering into the pool. A blue and white ceramic fountain adorns the wall facing it. In the fountain's bowl stands a little boy with the expected stream of water issuing from his genitals. Above the fountain hangs a sign: *We don't drink from your toilet. Please don't pee in our pool.*

I lift myself out and walk, dripping, to the tent. Peter greets me with, "Spaghetti OK?" I watch him stir a pot on the Coleman stove and smile—*Handsome!*

His face is so familiar—the straight nose, the soft mouth, the space between his two front teeth. His wavy grey hair has thinned, especially on top of his head. His brows are now also grey. Several deep lines chiselled in his forehead have always been there, it seems. Except for the laugh creases around his eyes, his deeply tanned face is still smooth. At least what I can see of it. His grey beard and moustache cover most of it. "You look like Moses," people tell him.

Peter's sense of humour plays itself out in many ways, including beard and moustache design. The moustache over the years has taken on many shapes: a thin line above his lip, a little vertical strip, a square patch like Hitler's, a full wide one, or one curled up at the ends like Captain Hook. "Oh, Hon," I'd say, "isn't that a little too far out for a principal?" He'd only laugh and work the end curls. The yearly school pictures tracked the changing patterns on his face—

long sideburns, goatee, full beard, or a thin line from moustache to a chin-only beard, like a Chinese person.

And then there were the mornings I'd notice something was different but wouldn't pay close attention. Suddenly a day or two later I'd blurt out, "You shaved off your beard!" As always, he would've kept track of how many hours it took for me to notice.

Sometimes I'd stare at an old school photo of him and wonder who the dark-haired youthful "stranger" was. The early childrearing years of our relationship often seemed like a blur.

But times have changed; he's changed. He's become much more "present" to me emotionally, something I hungered for in the early years. The last decade of our marriage especially has been good. The spaces in our relationship have gradually closed.

"Ready?" Peter's blue eyes sweep over to me. It's the eyes that remain the same. His eyes first made my heart beat faster. Windows to the soul—is that what makes them so attractive? Is the very essence of him reflected in his eyes—his forever-smiling eyes?

I take the plate of spaghetti, corned beef, and creamed corn he offers me. We bow our heads, and he thanks God for this beautiful day, for protection, for this special time together, for the kids back home, for our four little grandsons.

Yes, four! We recall the morning several weeks ago when Bruce called to say Diane had safely delivered their first-born—a beautiful baby boy. Peter excitedly collected dollar coins to use in the pay phone at night when the time was right to make a return call to Canada. (Jim and Julie's telephone wasn't hooked up yet after the move.)

"You annoyed us with that jingling of coins in your pocket all day," I remind him.

"A man with four grandsons has a right to be excited and jingle all he wants!" he replies with a proud grin.

After supper we settle down to read. No TV, no radio, no people, no noise. Only us in the stillness of the never-ending scrubby landscape.

"I'm going for a walk," Peter says and disappears from view behind a slight dip in the ground. I'm soon engrossed in Nevil Shute's novel *A Town Like Alice.*

"I saw graves back there." Peter startles me. "A child, and a young woman of twenty-eight, and others." He pauses. "It must've been lonely; probably no doctor."

Part of me resents this intrusion—not the intrusion into my reading as much as the intrusion of death into this lovely day. The kangaroos were enough.

"Yes, it must've been," I say without looking up. He continues to stand beside me as if he wants to continue the conversation, but I ignore him. He then folds himself into his chair and writes postcards to the kids.

At the beginning of his retirement, Peter bought a book about death. He asked several people to join him to discuss the book. No one was interested. No, we don't want to talk about death.

But, the subject *has* been brought up—again, and I've lost my concentration.

One day, during our visit at Jim's in Palm Cove, a mobile library parked on one of the residential streets. Peter was eager to have a look, and we entered the narrow trailer lined with books. I was disappointed in the selection but managed to find a novel and a book of Australian poetry. Peter was much more excited.

"Look what I found!" He held out three small volumes and, grinning, read the titles to me. *Leave it to him to find books on death!*

Incredulously, I asked, "Where did you find *those*?"

"In there," was his bemused answer.

The first of Peter's cache was *A Time to Love, A Time to Mourn* (Dixon). As he read it, he began to tell me the story: five siblings, the same order and ages as ours, deal with the terminal illness and death of one of them.

"The children must read this," he kept saying.

"The living and the dying can't really understand each other," he commented another day. "They're on completely different wavelengths."

Next book. Peter came into our bedroom at Jim and Julie's one morning with a cup of tea for me in one hand, the book in the other. "You must read this," he said. "It's the story of a widow and how she copes after her husband's death."

"I don't want to. Thanks for the tea. What are we doing today?"

Peter didn't give up. Again and again he suggested I read the book by Ingrid Trobisch, *Learning to Walk Alone.* One morning he looked deeply into my eyes and seriously said, "I *want* you to read this book."

I stubbornly refused. "I'm on holidays. I don't want to dwell on that now."

Yet still another morning, book and tea in hand, he said, "Do you want to hear how Walter died?"

"No."

He ignored my answer and continued. "Walter got up one morning, took a shower, made Ingrid a cup of tea, brought it to her in bed, sat down beside her, and just leaned back and died."

"Well, that's nice and tidy; maybe you could arrange that also."

I instantly regretted the flippant remark and the tone of my voice, so I picked up the book one morning while Peter was on his early morning stroll. Ingrid's story chronicles her struggle with widowhood. The stark reality of life lived alone pounded me square in the face and punctured holes in my flimsy, yet cozy blanket of denial. Peter returned to find me in tears.

"I can't ever go through what she went through," I cried. "I'm not strong like her. I can't cope like her."

Peter sat down on the bed and pulled me to him. I sobbed in his arms. He gently stroked my hair, my heaving shoulders. "Yes, you can," he murmured in my ear. "You'll be all right."

"No, I won't."

"You will. You *will* be all right." His voice broke with emotion.

He comforted; he encouraged; he understood; but a part of me felt it was easy for *him* to say those words. I needed to escape, deal with it on my own. I pulled my clothes on, said a hasty good morning to Jim and Julie, and mumbled something about going to the beach.

And that's where I spent the day—with the book—under the lonely palm at the far end of the beach where a creek empties into a small lagoon. I pulled my towel around the trunk of the tree as the sun slid the shade along. I read the book, cried, pounded the sand. A battle raged: a battle with fear; a battle with God. I felt as if I were swept along a tide I couldn't stop, pulled along a road I didn't wish to travel. And there was nothing I could do about it. Nothing. The road would lead to a precipice...

I reached the depth of it face down, sobbing into my towel.

Around 5 o'clock, exhausted, I trudged back home with a semblance of surrender, but also with sadness now lodged at a deeper level. We had a quiet meal. Maybe Peter told them. I sensed how deeply he respected my silence.

And then it was over. I watched Peter the next day, exuberant, full of energy, and thought it probably had been beneficial to break through more of my denial, to confront my fears, but nothing would happen with him being so well.

But the sadness remained.

Sunset

"Look at the sky." Peter's voice breaks the silence around us. My chair is facing east and I'm unaware of the display of colour behind me. We amble over the gravel to the road to get a full view of the extravagance of an outback sunset—the sky gone up in flame. All the red earth stretches out before us; the blush of the soil intensified with the slanting light of the setting sun so that it seems to glow. The spinifex balls are radiant with light. "Every common bush a fire...only he who sees takes off his shoes" (Browning).

Awed, we watch the drama of changing colour unfold. As if fighting against its descent, the ball of fire finally sinks behind a thin smudge of purple cloud just above the horizon.

"It's gone." Peter sighs softly.

But the sun is far from gone. Coloured tongues streak into the sky. They elongate to reach all around us. It's as if a glowing pumpkin veil is drawn up and over us. The motel's wall has been orange-washed; someone spilled dye in the pool. Fragments of sun-touched clouds float like bits of pink fluff on the east horizon. "Duds of emerald," Emily called them. "And now you've littered all the east / With duds of emerald!" (Dickinson).

The sky ripens to a deeper red, then darker still. We slowly walk back to the camper and sink into our chairs and into the silence of the evening. The gas lantern fizzes and hisses as Peter lights it and hangs it on a nail in the pole. We scoot our chairs close to gain the benefit of its dim light on our pages. A hushed, gentle darkness wraps itself around us.

"Look up." Peter's voice again, full of wonder. We rest our heads on the backs of our chairs and gaze at the sky, heavy with stars—a jet-black expanse of velvet punctured with light. Never have we seen stars so intense, so brilliant, seemingly so close. Peter scans the horizon and tries to figure out the southern constellations. "Where is the Southern Cross?" I ask.

"Don't know exactly. Close to the horizon, I think. We need to find the two bright stars that guide you to it," he adds as he adjusts his gaze.

It's a poetic night. Someone familiar with such an outback scene saw the stars as "altar fires." Later I look up the passage that gives this awesome night a voice: "When the white stars in reverence light their holy altar fires, and silence, like the touch of God, sinks deep into the breast" (George Essex Evans).

4

Behind the Back of Beyond

Wednesday, October 21

I wake to the sound of clinking cutlery. Peter greets me with "It's going to be a glorious day. Let's pack quickly and get on the road. I want to get to Mount Isa today."

"Mount Isa?" I question. "That's a long way!"

We're on our way by 6:30. Forty-five minutes later we meet the first car. We each swerve with two wheels onto the red dirt shoulders and send up the by now familiar cloud of dust. We're blending into the landscape. Red soil has lodged in all the cracks and crevices of the car's exterior, and since we have the windows rolled down most of the time, red dust has seeped into every nook and cranny of the interior as well. My denim purse looks as if streaked with rust; the white straps of my sandals look as if smeared with cumin. No matter what I touch, it's covered with red gritty dust.

We drive into Richmond in time for morning coffee. A clean looking café (they must have hosed it down) with red gingham curtains looks inviting. Inside, the same cloth covers small square tables. We make conversation with the elderly owner-waitress as she serves us delicious freshly brewed coffee. She tells us they moved into town after living on a cattle station all their married life.

"Do you like living here?" I ask.

"It's hard to get used to," she answers. "It's so busy."

I suppress a smile.

I now take the wheel and a half hour later a terrible smack startles us. One of the retreads has come undone. Peter tears the rest of the rubber off as best he can and we contemplate what to do: go on into the unknown or go back to a service station we saw in Richmond. We decide to retrace our steps. The service station has no tires, but the kind man directs us to the only other one in town. We count ourselves fortunate; we're on our way with a new tire within an hour and a half.

Our happy chattering continues as we drive out of Richmond, but gradually we grow quiet. The hum of the motor plays like background music in a silent elevator. The temperature is rising. It's hot inside the car. The road seems like an elastic band; it stretches further and further away from us.

I focus on the railway running alongside the road. At least there is another travel trail. A little cart has rolled by on the tracks. Several men standing on its platform, pumping bars to propel it forward, waved, friendly-like. They'd stop should we be stranded. But there is no shelter for them from the sun.

I hunger for noise, long to see a train. Its clamour would be a welcome sound—not frightening as at the campground yesterday morning. The clickity-clack of wheels, the long weeping sounds of a whistle, or the jubilant jingle of an old brass bell across this empty space; an ancient engine hissing and spouting steam as shiny copper pipes punch the wheels. A train from childhood days. As children we'd put our ears to the track and listen for the zing of the train long before it chugged around the bend. We'd lay a penny on the rails and watch as the steel wheels squished it into a paper-thin shiny disk. We watched people weep as they said goodbye at the station.

We take a lunch break in Julia Creek and drive on in the unrelenting, sweating heat. The railroad runs just south of the highway now but is out of view, and I miss its presence, its reassuring presence. I do see a row of trees in the distance south of us.

"Look, Hon, there are trees."

Peter looks and murmurs something.

"They look like soldiers shivering in a pool of water," I say.

"I keep seeing these oases in front of us, but we never get to them," he adds.

We grow quiet—busy with our own thoughts. The immense sun-blasted vastness around us is overwhelming, frightening. We're out of our element, reduced to a proper awareness of our fragility—two people, some clothes, a little food, some bottled water, an old car. What would happen should we have car trouble beyond a faulty tire? How long could we last, broiling under this fiery sun?

The hot, dry wind burns my eyes. I pinch towels into the top of the windows to shade us, leaving only the side vents open for air. With little air, the car becomes like an oven.

I splash moisturizer on my face and hands; my skin will look wrinkled and aged before we ever get through this desert. I crawl into the back seat, wanting to shut out the harsh brightness of the sun, the long stretch of road ahead. I close my eyes; they sting. I try to doze; I can't. I long for coolness, moisture. The longing prods my mind to linger on a memory—the day Jim and Julie took us for a stroll in the moist, cool rainforest.

Mossman Rainforest

Jim led the way on the narrow path alongside the Mossman River. The path led us away from the water, deeper and deeper into the dark, damp stillness of the rainforest. The trees closed in behind us and we were in a world apart—a world secluded and silent, yet throbbing, pulsating with life.

An assortment of foreign bird whistles and warbles echoed continuously throughout the rainforest with their antiphony of praise.

Leaves rustled as a small creature skittered away at our feet. A branch crackled; a leaf zigzagged past; an animal called. Hushed, we let the music of the forest penetrate.

We craned our necks to see the massive trees high overhead fight shoulder-to-shoulder for space. A thick canopy of myriad shadowed leaves blotted out the blue sky. Thick strangler vines, stretching from the top of this world to the earth beneath, encircled trunks and branches. A variety of plants were rooted on the great lengths of the trunk. It made them look like giant mothers nursing a long string of adopted children.

Peter pointed out the orchids—dark mauve, delicate cream—nestled in the cracks and crotches of the trees. Green ferns bowed gracefully high above our heads. Shiny leaves dripped droplets of moisture and gave credibility to the term *rain* forest.

The air smelled moist and earthy, and we inhaled it deeply as we whispered about the miracle of this perfectly balanced ecosystem so alive for untold ages. We took turns carrying Dylan and pointing to all the wonders we saw.

Slowly we made our way back to the river and Peter noticed a thick vine dangling above the shaded, shallow water. He glanced up and tugged on it. Believing it was firmly attached, he grasped it and swung, Tarzan-like, over the river and back, adding his own jubilant cry to the sounds of the forest. We cheered when he landed safely, but we couldn't be coaxed to follow.

Reluctantly, we meandered out of the forest back into the brightness of this sun-drenched land.

2 p.m.

A tiny town—a cluster of buildings dignified by a name. A service station. A shower. I stand in line to wait my turn.

"Have a shower, Hon," I encourage.

"No, I want to get going."

Why is he rushing so?

"We'll stop for a break in the next town," he promises.

Cloncurry, the next town, is a sizeable place. The welcome sign informs us it's the home of the Royal Flying Doctor Service founded by John Flynn in 1928. We read a bit about this great man, a true

Australian saint, who also found lonely graves in the outback distressing, and worked to provide a "mantel of safety" to the wilderness. Heart-wrenching stories of need spurred him on to establish a flying doctor service to the people in the great outback.

One such story involved a young husband travelling toward Cloncurry with his pregnant wife in order for her to receive medical assistance during her delivery. It started to rain. The red earth turned to mud. The cart's wheels sank down. The young wife delivered her baby on a blanket on the mud. Both mother and baby died and the young man had to dig a grave in the mud to bury his family.

I shudder and push the scene away. We're not in the mood to visit the Flying Doctor's site—we're looking for shade in order to have a rest.

"There is a tree; that would do."

"You call that shade?" Peter's voice tinged with sarcasm. All the other trees are smaller, and we start to argue about square footage of shade! Our nerves are wearing thin.

Suddenly, we hear children's voices and happy laughter. We turn a corner and before us is a public swimming pool! We dive into the blue cool water but swim in silence.

3 p.m.

We've been on the road nine long hours today, and it's more than enough, but Peter's plan is to get to Mount Isa and we drive further into the outback, further into the sizzling heat.

Our guidebook tells us that to see the twin smokestacks of the Mount Isa mines in the distance is sheer relief for the desert traveller. I stare across the empty, motionless landscape. It gradually changes, and the road takes us through rolling, rocky hills. Finally, I see two tall, thin needles take shape on the distant hazy horizon. Very slowly, the needles thicken. We climb another grade and trees appear, greener grass grows along the road, and we see smoke rise from the tall chimneys. Straight columns, seemingly pulled from the cylinders, unfold and lazily billow like lengths of flimsy grey gauze that slowly dissipate.

It's 6 o'clock when Mount Isa becomes a reality.

We see a caravan park on our right before we enter the town proper.

"I guess this is as good as any," Peter mumbles.

He registers and drives to a spot along the back fence. "This OK?"

"Yeah, sure." Our words are few.

I check for railroad tracks. There are none.

We cook our *tea*, read a bit.

"I'm going to bed." Obviously dead tired, Peter crawls into the camper. It's still stifling hot. I decide it'd be better to sleep outside on the *chaise*.

A group of motorcyclists pitch their tents nearby. They seem to be celebrating a reunion by the sounds of it. Their boisterous *yarning* and peals of laughter punch through the silence of the evening. The racket is annoying. I hope they'll all retire shortly. They have no such plan.

Midnight

It's dark. There are no "altar fires." The lights of the town, as well as a thin cloud cover, have hidden the stars. I'm restless. We're only two days into our journey—another two or three to Alice Springs— then another similar stretch to Adelaide. *What possessed us? And why the breakneck speed?*

I toss and turn and try to shut out the noise of our neighbours. I can't. And I also can't shut out the noise that is all of me just now.

They say we bring nothing into the desert only to find we've brought it all. I've brought all I am to this God-forsaken place—my anxiety, fear, anger, lack of faith.

An ominous darkness blankets me.

I try to shake it off.

It keeps oozing back.

It claws at me.

I wrestle with it.

I try to pray. God seems so remote.

44

The weight of the threatening cloud that has hung over my life—our lives—the last few years presses in, throttles. My mind is on replay. Grim images appear in quick succession. The times he was late coming home, the fear, the nightmares—the core always the same: it's night...heart attack...telephone is dead...need to run to the neighbours...can't find my clothes...can't get them on...they don't fit...I lose the precious minutes that decide between life and death—I wake, heart pounding.

Why this suffocating gloom? Have I plummeted into a pit of grief? Didn't I face my fears on the beach in Palm Cove? Didn't I surrender the fear as best I knew how? Why does it grip me so tonight? This sinister blackness—is this what Saint John of the Cross calls "the dark night of the soul"?
There's not a ray of light. I've lost my way.

I sob into my pillow.

"You must go back to school," Peter said years ago. "Prepare for when you'll be alone." I went to school, got the job, prepared—everything is ready. Nothing is ready. How preposterous to think one can be ready to be torn in two, ready to have your heart ripped out. *I'm too young. It's not fair!*

1 a.m.

The raucous laughter mocks me—makes sport of my fear.

I sit up, take deep breaths of the warm night air. Desperate to console myself, I listen to Peter's measured breathing. He's so strong, can drive all day, has no pain.

And there's the promise: "...rise on the wings of the dawn...settle on the far side of the sea...your right hand will hold me...."

We'll be safe. God promised.

2 a.m.

The slurred voices are intermittent now; the laughter slowly dies. The night becomes still.

But there are no "altar fires."

5

Refining Fires

We sleep in, wake to our usual camping routine: breakfast, tidy up. It's another brilliant sunlit morning. We plan the day.

"I think it would be interesting to tour the mines. I could walk to the information booth and see when the tours are."

"Why don't you," Peter says. "I'll pack and get the car serviced."

"I'll be back in an hour," I say, grateful the night has healed our raw emotions.

I walk to the gate and turn onto a dirt footpath that runs alongside the road. The campground owner swings out the gate beside me and offers me a ride in his truck. He's friendly and inquires about us.

"Are you coping with the heat? It'll be another hot one. It's 40 C already," he offers. I'm shocked. It's only 9:30.

The kind man drops me off at the information booth. I'm told there is a two-hour bus tour of the mines at 1 o'clock. I pick up pamphlets and slowly retrace my steps along the dusty path back to the campground. It *is* hot. I feel the sun burning my arms. I slip into the long-sleeved shirt I brought along for protection.

I find our camper neatly packed up. *Great, Peter will be back shortly.* I settle in the shade of a tree and read the mine tour brochure.

Time passes. The shade is so thin it doesn't really shield. An hour passes. Our books are locked in the camper; so are paper and pencil. I have nothing to do except read the brochure. I've now committed to memory that the Mount Isa mine is the largest gold, silver, copper, and zinc mine in the world. *Well, yippee!*

I get a drink, walk around a bit, but it's too hot. Better to sit still.

Another hour passes. The familiar fear lurks like a shadowy shape. Must not let it enter my space, let it get the best of me.

Where is he? Do I need to find him?

After nearly three hours, I anxiously decide to walk back into town. As I approach the gate, our car enters it. Peter sticks his head out the window but before he can say anything I blurt out, "Where *were* you? You *know* how upsetting it is not to know where you are! Where *were* you?"

"Didn't you know it would take awhile to service the car?" he quietly says.

Service? Shamefaced, I realize I'd thought only of a fill-up.

I slide into the car, and we drive into town.

"I found a beautiful air-conditioned mall, and I'd rather spend the afternoon there than sitting in a bus," Peter says. "So you go ahead and enjoy the mine tour and meet me at the mall. I'll find you."

He drops me off at the info booth and wishes me a good time.

I climb into a grand air-conditioned bus with roomy plush seats and for the next two hours am entertained by an Aussie bus driver/tour guide who freely and humorously shares all he knows about the Mount Isa mines: 140 kilometres of railroad, 200 tons of machinery, vats of blistering molten metals, all down in the bowels of the earth.

At the end of the tour, the bus makes a slow turn around a corner of one of the large metal sheds. In the yard before us, filled with a variety of vehicles, piles of wood and other nondescript stuff, something glitters in the sun. The bus pulls closer, stops, and in a soft dramatic voice our guide announces: "And there is the gold."

A communal gasp travels the length of the bus. Two piles of gold bricks, each at least two metres square, neatly stacked on skids, stand before us in all their deep-yellow gleaming glory. They look like golden altars. Every angle and corner a playground for the bright desert sun, they blind us, leave us speechless. So much gold, so much preciousness extracted from this rugged emptiness. How many bricks are just sitting there, outside, in the middle of the yard, so casually, so nonchalantly, as if someone were ready to use them to pave a sidewalk!

We stare at the lustrous stacks and finally find our voices and pelt the driver with questions. Who guards the gold? What is the value? Is it transported by train? Who guards the train? The bus driver chuckles and patiently answers our queries. Then he slowly backs up, and we leave the golden mounds proudly mirroring the sun.

But the gold doesn't leave me that easily.

I think of a passage a friend and I shared during a difficult time. "I will give you the treasures of darkness…" (Isaiah 45:3). This great treasure of gold was wrested somehow from the earth's dark belly. Last night was so dark…it seems impossible to think of a treasure somewhere.

And the piles looked like altars.

I glance at the mine's tall chimneys, the dominant feature of this town. Smoke is steadily rising; furnaces are burning; the refining fire—blue-hot fire. Job said when God is finished with him he'll come forth as gold. I think of my fear last night, my angry frustration this morning.

Tears well up. *There's still so much dross, Lord—will there ever be any gold?*

I pass the bus depot on my way to the mall to meet Peter and see a few large buses lined up. They look so attractive, now that I know how cool and comfortable they are. *What if I took a bus for a short while?* It might give us both a bit of a break.

Large glass doors transport me from a hot dust-covered world to the cool, clean environment of the mall. The contrast takes me by surprise and for a moment I stare in disbelief at this totally different world.

Peter is walking toward me, the familiar grin on his face.

"Isn't this great? Did you enjoy the mine tour?"

I tell him some of the interesting facts, the stacks of gold and then say, "I've got an idea."

As if not hearing me he says, "I've been thinking. Why don't you take the bus to Alice Springs while I drive the camper there?"

"That was my idea!" I say with surprise. Maybe we're on the same page, after all. "It's a long way to Alice. I thought of taking it just for a couple of hours–to the next stop.

"It's a night bus; just take it."

"Will you be all right?"

"Yes, of course."

"I'll check in at one of the hostels, so look for me there."

"I'll find you," he answers confidently.

He drives me to the bus station as he's anxious to be on the road. We hug each other goodbye and Peter says, "I'll see you in two days, Saturday around suppertime."

I watch him as he slowly drives away.

7 p.m.

Only a dozen or so passengers board the bus, so there is plenty of seating space. Everyone can take at least two seats to curl up on for the night's journey. I choose the left front double seat to have full view of the road. I'll be looking for a camper trailer pulled by a grey Toyota and wonder when we'll overtake it.

The bus departs and soon hums along. The radio blares harshly, not my kind of music. I hope we'll lose the station. We don't. My eyes are peeled on the lonely road. We pass a few vehicles.

The sun has set–it's dark. I peer out the window into the black-ness beyond the small circle of yellow light shed by the headlights, convinced I'll still be able to distinguish the Toyota and camper.

I wonder about the darkness I felt last night while Peter slept so peacefully. He's so much at peace, journeys so joyfully. He claims joy as his right, finds it where others see hardship and

49

adversity. He ecstatically announced on his birthday last year, "I now have lived as long as my dad did."

11 p.m.

We arrive at the Barkly roadhouse, a travellers' pit stop, a place to camp overnight. The passengers disembark to stretch, to buy a snack. I'm not hungry and anxiously walk around to the back of the roadhouse. Among the half a dozen cars and several caravans parked for the night I expect to find Peter, but at a glance, I see he's not there. I wander around the yard willing him to be there. *Where is he? Why didn't he stop here for the night? I could've joined him here.*

Discouraged, I climb back into the bus, and we roll further into the black night. Fragments of a passage come to mind. "Watchman, what is left of the night?" The answer puzzled me and does so even now. The watchman replies, "Morning is coming, but also the night" (Isaiah 21:11,12). It's another three hours to the roadhouse at Three Ways. The Barkly Highway ends there to meet the Stuart Highway that runs north/south across this vast continent. (Some years later the Barkly Highway was realigned to meet the Stuart Highway south of the roadhouse.)

I expect Peter will have stopped at Three Ways.

The radio station crackles, fades, and thankfully is turned off—but I can't sleep.

My idea of taking the bus does not sit too well any more. With heavy eyes, I stare into the night.

2 a.m.

The bus approaches the deserted roadhouse at Three Ways. I expect it to pull in, but to my dismay, it doesn't. It drives past the seemingly deserted building to where the two highways meet in a T shape. The roadhouse is nestled in the left corner of the T, so as the bus turns left (south) onto the Stuart Highway, I thankfully have full view of what looks like the front of the building. The yard is dimly lit but enough for me to see that our Toyota is not among the few cars parked there.

Where is he? How could I have missed him? He was nowhere on that road. I scoured every inch.

With tears stinging, I lean my head against the window and finally doze off. Twenty-five kilometres later, the bus grinds to a stop in Tenant Creek. All passengers going to Alice Springs have to transfer to another bus.

Now on a different, clean bus, I huddle into myself on the roomy seats and finally sleep.

6

Alice Springs

Friday, October 23
4:30 a.m.

The bus slows and stops. It's still dark, but I see an Aborigine family waiting at the side of the road. They board the bus, huddle close together, and we drive on.

The eastern sky, brushed with the faintest pink, beckons me to stay awake and watch God make a morning. The landscape is the same—spinifex balls dot the ground like porcupines. Dry tufts of grass, scraggly bushes, a thirsty eucalyptus are all enhanced by the gentle glow of dawn on this arid plain. I can just make out where a long dusky red driveway leads to some remote cattle station. It reminds me of the lady in the gingham café missing life in the outback—missing "the everlasting sameness of the never-ending plains" (Evans). They say the outback hooks one into its silence, into the simplicity of life, so much so that one is loath to leave. I'm beginning to appreciate more and more the stark silent beauty of this vast wilderness.

A new day. The light of dawn chases away some of the shadows in my soul. Peter is wherever he is. We'll meet tomorrow in Alice. He said he'd find me.

I'm disappointed that we passed the Devil's marbles while I was asleep. Early surveyors spoke of this part of the outback as Devil's country. When they came upon the stretch of granite rock eroded into rounded shapes of all sizes, strewn around in piles, one of them commented that it looked as if the Devil himself had emptied a bag of marbles.

A few hours later, I wake to see a shadowed mountain range far off in the distance. It stretches out before us like a solid dark barricade. The MacDonnell Ranges. Alice Springs will be nestled somewhere along its base. The mountain range consists of tiers of solid red rock, broken in places by gaps, gorges, chasms or canyons carved out over time. The largest gap is just wide enough to allow the Todd River, the Stuart Highway, and a railroad to pass through the mountain like three threads through the eye of a needle. A spring within the river was named Alice, after Todd's wife. The town of Alice Springs was built a few kilometres from the spring. I strain to catch a glimpse, but I can't see until we're quite close. No highrises to mark her presence on the desert floor.

Nevil Shute, in *A Town Like Alice,* refers to her as a *bonza town.* I've come to feel a strange affection for her, this spring in the desert. Many a weary traveller has been refreshed here. I hope our time with her—in her—will also be a time of renewal.

10 a.m.

The bus pulls into Alice Springs and parks at the Ford Plaza. In a telephone book I locate the address of the Sandrifter Safari Lodge, a fancy name for the most basic of accommodations. I'm in camping mode and don't even consider a cool hotel room. I walk down Todd Street, past shops, banks, a tourist bureau, airline offices and a typical ornate Aussie hotel with its two-storeyed veranda skirting front and sides. A footbridge takes me across the wide, waterless Todd River. Cars drive through the river here on the road that merely dips down across the red sand riverbed and continues up the other side. They call the Todd the *upside-down river.* Water runs somewhere beneath the sandy surface. Majestic white-barked ghost gums and desert gums grow along the banks as well as in the middle of the river, speaking of an unseen water source below. To think of this river as a torrent after a sudden desert storm is almost unbelievable.

At the lodge, I book into the last room available, a small space with a cot, a desk, a chair, and a tiny square closet. I shower, find an oversized sink outside under a sheet metal roof labelled "laundry area," and wash the red dust and bus odour from my clothes.

After a nap, I walk back to the plaza. On the footbridge across the Todd River, I meet a backpacker who was also on the bus. We recognize each other and stop to chat. She says, "I keep hearing about the Todd River, but I can't find it. Do you know where it is?"

"You're standing on it," I reply, enjoying her expression of disbelief, and we chuckle over the concept of the upside-down river.

At the mall, I buy a can of beans and sit on a bench to watch the people. The sound of water spraying from a tall fountain creates a soothing background, softening the shoppers' chatter and clatter of shoes. A profusion of tropical plants huddled in hefty planters enhances the shiny clean space. A wide staircase leads to a mezzanine above and a curtain of green vines cascades down from the second-storey balustrade. On the opposite side, high above the shops, a row of squat windows lets daylight spill inside. A small photo kiosk and a larger souvenir kiosk stand in the middle of the walking space. I take note of some of the shops and a large cafeteria in which to buy a meal.

Another day and night before Peter will be here. I'm bored. I miss him. In my absent-mindedness, I see someone approach who looks familiar. Is my mind playing tricks? It looks like…but it can't be; he's not to arrive until tomorrow. But it *is* Peter! He looks different. Oh, it's the beard; it's gone again. He has utterly surprised me and stands before me, smiling, eyes alight with amusement. His smile ripples through me like a tickle and relief floods me like the sunshine pouring in through the high windows.

"When did you get here?" I finally ask.

"I arrived two hours after the bus. I saw you pass in the night."

"You drove all night?"

"I slept an hour between five and six this morning." Then hastily he adds, "And I had a good nap after I got here."

Strange how I looked for him all night, searched for him to no avail, yet he saw me.

"I found a great place to camp. Come, I'll show you."

I follow and am so thankful I don't have to eat my beans alone. We drive out of town onto Larapinta Drive.

"Guess what my big adventure was," Peter asks, smiling.

"What?"

"I saw twenty-four kangaroos!"

"That many?"

"Yes. Two came out to walk across the road. I didn't hit them," he adds, relieved.

"I'm glad. Did you see the Devil's marbles?"

"Yes. The road cuts right through them. It's an amazing heap of stone."

We make a right turn into the Stuart Caravan Park. The campground is like a small forest and we grow quiet as the car slowly finds its way under the foliage. Peter stops beside a large tree. Our site, like all the others, is enclosed on three sides by a double row of logs sitting upon stubby uprights. It creates a room-like feeling. The tree's branches reach protectively over our camper—its leaves provide shade from the now sinking sun. The sites around us are unoccupied; a few silver metal caravans are parked further along under the trees. No one is around; we have the place to ourselves.

After supper, Peter lights the lantern; we have a cup of tea, chat and plan to stay put for a few days.

When it's bedtime I say, "I'd like to sleep at the lodge tonight. All my things are there and I'd like the experience."

"Of course; take the car and go ahead. I'll see you in the morning."

I slowly drive out of the grounds, find my way back to the lodge, and sleep well on the narrow bed.

7

High Places

I drive back to the caravan park, feeling light and happy. With the stress of this part of the journey behind us, we'll plan to have a nice holiday here in Alice. I consider discussing our time in Mount Isa, our disagreements about how to travel through this desert, but then I think, *Everything is fine now; why bring it up?* A wiser part of me prods: *bring it up; clean it up.*

I drive into the park and find our spot and Peter waiting for me to enjoy this day together.

Tentatively I say, "I don't relish spending any more days like the ones we've had."

"Me neither."

We talk. It's one of those rare occasions when one can be completely honest, completely kind, and feel completely understood. I need to be reassured that we won't travel like maniacs across this desert, that we'll have frequent stops and shorter days. Peter needs for me to trust him, as he also wants to arrive safely in Adelaide.

I playfully say, "Write me a note."

We each sit down to write; I fill a page in my spiral notebook and tear it out. Peter is still writing. Finally, he tears off six sheets with one deft movement and hands them to me, eyes twinkling. I joyfully accept his gift, his love, his embrace.

"Let's go; we have a lot to explore. I've already made us a sandwich and a thermos of tea for our lunch," Peter says excitedly.

We drive around a bit in Alice to get our bearings and then go to the spring from which she derived her name. The spot is a historical reserve—a telegraph station carved out of the wilderness to relay every overseas cable message and newspaper story from Darwin to Adelaide, one letter at a time in Morse code. The old building is a large square stone structure with deep small windows and a wide veranda all around to deflect the summer sun's hot rays.

We walk down a long slope of sand to the water—the spring—no more than a water hole in the dry Todd River. Gum trees and desert oaks shade the calm, serene pool of water. On the opposite side a sheer rock cliff rises out of the water. How often did a lonely homemaker come to sit by these waters, draw strength and comfort from the tranquil charm in order to continue to live in the *back of beyond*?

We return to Larapinta Drive and head west along the bareboned, bare-swept russet mountain range. It's nearly lunchtime, and Peter suggests we find a spot to have a picnic. We meander onto a lane and come upon a spot where one giant white gum straddles a dry creek bed.

"Perfect place," Peter says excitedly. We carefully spread our lunch on the fat fallen trunk and perch ourselves on each side. It takes a little balancing, but we manage and giggle about our perfect picnic table.

We drive on in search of John Flynn's gravesite. It's not difficult to find the grave, as there is really nothing out here except sand and rock and a few trees. A gate and chain garland cordon off the site. The gate is open and we walk up the slight rise to a simple base of quartzite stone topped by a Devil's Marble.

I read the inscription on the base: "Beneath this stone rest the ashes…"

My throat constricts.

Time skips back…

We were walking home from Palm Cove Beach in the late afternoon when suddenly Peter turned to me and said, "If anything happens to me I want to be cremated here and I want you to stay here until you are ready to fly home." One complete long sentence, obviously well thought out. I didn't comment—just dismissed the statement...

Now it's staring me in the face. "Beneath this stone rest the ashes..."

We seem to be looking at graves a lot.

We walk around the area, almost reverently. A trio of white-barked ghost gums is all that adorns the rocky, sandy space, but they stand like a gleaming white sentry keeping watch.

Peter exclaims how huge the eight-ton boulder is that tops the grave. He wants a photo with both of us in it, and walks back to the gate to perch the camera on one of the posts. He then runs back to the grave. It's a long run and only part of him is in the picture.

We continue our drive westward that will lead us to the drama of gaps and chasms, gorges and canyons in the mountain range. Someone must have been so impressed with the formations in the rocky range that they used all the words in the thesaurus to describe the phenomenon of spaces carved out in the rock over eons of time.

Simpson's Gap is the first stop. It's one of the larger gaps and has a small pool of water between the pink rock walls that rise and widen at the top. Two white gums grow close by and I centre them in the V-shaped gap as I focus my camera to take a photo. Peter decides he must take a picture from the other side and tries to scramble across the water, balancing against the rock walls. Of course, he loses his footing and ends up with a soaker, but he gets across, to the delight of the few people present. He asks a lady in a red blouse to please be in all his pictures to add a spot of colour. He scrambles back safely to this side and continues to take photos of the rock formations.

"Look up there; do you see that?"

"What?"

"Up there, isn't that beautiful?"

"I don't see anything."

"The rock, look at the way the shadow contrasts the colour."

"Oh, there! Yes."

He calls me again. "Look, up there!"

It's only a mountain of rock, Peter.

He points to a protrusion. "Isn't that amazing?"

It's all a mass of chiselled pinkish rock. The direction of the sun's rays creates many light and shadow patterns and the blush of the rock changes with the amount of light shed on it. He's so taken with the simple rugged splendour of it all–I only see a mountain of rock.

He points again. "Look, way up high. Do you see it?"

"You mean the rock?"

"No, something else, right there. Do you see it?"

I focus my gaze along his finger and finally see what he sees, a rock wallaby, standing proud and tall at the edge of a cliff. As if he knows we're watching him, he suddenly bounds away, surefooted on the rocky heights.

"Hind's feet on high places," Peter mutters (Hurnard).

We wander around and suddenly he comes toward me with a long snake dangling across a pole!

"Don't be afraid; it can't hurt you; its head has been crushed."

He picks it up by the tip of its tail and holds it high. The snake's head reaches the ground and, powerless, slightly curls up. The few children present gather around and receive a lesson in snake lore. I watch Peter's generous smile and wonder about his joy today. His laughter rings out and echoes on the rock.

We drive on to Standley Chasm, but the gate closes in front of us. There's only a native *dingo* who stares at us as if to say, "Ha, you missed it."

6 p.m.

Back in Alice Springs, Peter suggests we drive up Anzac Hill to watch the sunset. The top of the small hill is level; several wooden benches stand around the perimeter. They afford magnificent views of Alice with the mountain range behind and the never-ending expanse of red earth in other directions. A white stone war monument surrounded by a garland of fat chain-link commands attention; it's a simple monolith set in a square stone base all gleaming white, etched with names.

A gentleman has brought a carload of Aborigine children up the hill tonight. He banters with them, a happy talkative bunch, and I look around to see where Peter is, as he's usually the first to join a conversation where children are present. He's standing at the war memorial. One foot is placed on the thick chain; his elbow rests on his lifted knee; and his chin is cupped in his hand. I wander over to him.

"Look at the names," he says pensively. "All young men who only lived a short while."

"Yes," I say, as I read some of the names, noting the early age of death.

He holds my eyes in an uncharacteristic way. His voice comes softly as if from a deep inner part. "I was promised ten years after my surgery. I've had nearly twenty; what more do I want?"

The question hangs between us. There's a light in his eyes as he continues to look at me and as I continue my silence. He sighs and softly says, "Let's sit on a bench to watch the sunset."

He chooses a west-facing bench and clicks the shutter repeatedly to capture the deepening colours in the sky as the red-hot globe slowly slides down to the horizon.

I'm restless and wander around.

"Come sit here," Peter says, "I want to take some silhouettes of you."

He directs me to another bench and focuses my profile against the flaming sky.

"Enough," I say.

"No, look, the sky is continually changing."

I get up again to walk around, but again he asks me to sit with him. I finally settle beside him and together we watch the beauty of the reds turn to mauves and purples and darker still. A native artist, Albert Namatjira, mixed a purple on his palette that echoed the purple of the evening hills; it was dubbed *Namatjira purple*.

Peter's arm is around my shoulders. Everyone has gone. Darkness seeps into the sky. Only the smallest smudge of colour remains at the far-off horizon.

"It's dark. It's over. Let's go."

"No," he says, "it's not over. Turn around."

I turn my head and gasp to see a dazzling scene below—Alice twinkling with light.

"Look, the City of Light," he whispers with deep emotion.

Some thoughts can't be wrapped in words. Silent, we gaze at the contrasting scenes. As the darkness increases, the town, like a many-faceted jewel, sparkles more and more brightly. Alone on this hill, we drink in the evening's exquisite beauty, laden with meaning.

Finally, hand in hand, we walk back to the car and drive to the campground, still silent, still spellbound by the magic of the evening.

Something tugs at the hem of my thoughts, but I'm not willing to pay heed, not willing to contemplate anything except that this has been an extraordinary day—with an even more extraordinary evening.

8

A Glimpse of Glory

Sunday, October 25

Peter's joyful voice wakes me with "Tea's ready!" Then, "Let's hurry so we can drive around town to find a church to attend."

I slip into my clothes and blink in the early morning light.

"Come on, wake up," he teases.

We eat our simple breakfast of cold cereal, toast, and tea, drive into Alice, and methodically navigate our way to several churches located in different parts of town. We arrive back on Todd Street and look for a spot to have a cup of coffee. The town is extremely quiet; virtually no one is about. I look at my wrist and see I forgot my watch.

"What time is it?"

"Eight o'clock," Peter answers, triumphantly awaiting my reaction.

"Only eight o'clock? You got me up this early on a Sunday morning?"

He laughs his hearty laugh. "There are too many things to do to sleep the time away!"

Well, we have lots of time to sit here at this little table covered with a cheery red-checked cloth, sip coffee and watch people. A few are now strolling by.

The John Flynn Memorial Uniting Church, a beautiful natural-stone structure built in memory of Australia's truest "saint," is directly across the street.

"We might as well attend there," Peter says.

It looks inviting, with large open windows, a water garden and generous plantings. We're one of the first to enter and choose a pew close to the front. It's cool and bright inside and I'm caught up in the cheerful atmosphere—maybe it's Peter's exuberance that fills this place. He eagerly receives a bulletin and reads every word of it. He opens his Bible, fishes a pencil out of his pocket, and starts to under-line something with strong, deft strokes so characteristic of his "teacher marking" style. He nudges me, eyes sparkling.

"I'm going to see Daniel. Look."

He points to the back of the bulletin. It has Psalm 128 printed out in full. He has his Bible open to the same psalm and now points to verse 6, which he's just heavily underlined: "...and may you live to see your children's children."

"See? It's a promise. I *am* going to see Daniel. Daniel Peter." He says the names with emotion—our fourth grandson, bearing his name.

I observe Peter out of the corner of my eye. The teacher-preacher, always dressed smartly in suit and tie on Sunday morn-ings, sitting here dressed in white shorts, pink T-shirt, bare feet in floppy black thongs. He couldn't look more casual.

Rev. Douglas Turnbull leads us in a joyful service that includes the baptism of baby Michelle. He holds her tenderly and says, "We have received little Michelle into God's and our family today. She's unaware of this, so we're going to covenant together to love her, to guide her and teach her about the Saviour, so that, when she's of age, she'll understand and accept Him as her own. Now meet little Michelle."

He steps down from the podium and, carrying the baby as if she were his own, he slowly walks down and back up the aisle, stopping now and then as people spontaneously reach out to touch the little one. The tender scene moves me to tears.

Tea and coffee are served outside after the service and Peter mingles happily. He talks to Doug, the minister, and asks directions to the youth centre where the announced Aborigine service will be held tonight at 6:30.

We saunter over to the Ford Plaza. The stores are closed, except for the Australian Artifact Shop. Peter's eye catches a pile of kangaroo skins.

"I should get one. I really should."

We lift the skins one by one, admiring the shades of brown and red in the lovely soft fur. He pulls one out of the pile.

"This one is perfect."

He pays the cashier and leaves the shop, happy with his purchase.

The souvenir kiosk is also open, and we browse. I find two T-shirts. One says: *I climbed Ayers Rock. Impressed?* The other reads: *I didn't climb the Rock—so what?*

"Look, Hon, a shirt for each of us," I say.

"What makes you think I'm not going to climb the Rock?" he answers, his voice tinged with a note of disdain.

We have lunch in the cafeteria and Peter pulls the kangaroo skin out of the bag to have another look.

"You're so happy," I comment.

"Well, wouldn't you be if you were going to a family reunion?"

"Family reunion?"

"Yes, when we get to Adelaide I'll see my niece whom I haven't seen for years, and my sister whom I haven't seen for six weeks. Wouldn't you be happy?"

"Yes, of course."

(But it seems to me the exuberance exceeds the occasion.)

We find a park near the youth centre where we relax for the afternoon.

"There's a group of Aborigines. I'm going over to talk with them. Want to come?" he asks.

"No, I prefer to just sit here."

I watch as he joins the circle. He sits down with them and soon laughter floats across the park. I remember similar occasions.

While we camped in Townsville last week, we spent some time in a park. Several Aborigines came up to us and asked Peter to help an illiterate lady fill out a form to obtain a flat. He guided them and entertained the group with his English instruction. Their laughter rang across that park also, and I wondered how it was they'd approached him for help.

Now he walks back to me.

"Look what I bought!" he exclaims as he shows me two strings of beads.

"They were so interesting, asked me all about Canada and things."

We walk to the youth centre in time for the Aboriginal service. We create a study in black and white—a white, white-haired man in white shorts among thirty or so black people. Terry Medley, who will lead the service, warmly welcomes us at the door and asks Peter if he'd be so kind as to say a few words, bring a greeting from "overseas."

After some hearty singing, Peter walks to the front and, always conscious of children present, he begins with, "Boys and girls, have you ever seen a bird in a cage or a dog fenced in a pen? What happens when you open the gate?" He waits a moment, spreads his arms wide and, with a glow on his face, he answers the question. "They're free!" He says the words with deep emotion and I feel a shiver run up my spine. He continues and, in a most animated manner, tells us about the freedom we can have in Christ, and the perfect freedom we'll experience one day with Him in heaven. He speaks so simply, yet so convincingly. His face radiates.

He sits back down beside me and I lean over and whisper, "Where did you get that?"

He looks at me quizzically. "Get what?"

"What you said."

"What do you mean?"

I realize he's completely unaware of the impact he has made.

After the service, Terry chats with us and invites us to come and visit him tomorrow at the caravan where he lives in the Amoonguna Aboriginal Community.

We slowly find our way back to our campground. Peter lights the lantern and we pull our chairs close to the light, me to read, Peter to write postcards to the children and to the staff at two schools at which he used to be the principal. I read a bit, then reach for my journal and reflect on our days here in Alice: *We're so happy, so much in love—we seem to literally float through the days. We're in a good place, a very good place…*

Suddenly, Peter says, "I want to phone the boys."

"Really? We decided not to call home unless there's an emergency."

"I want to talk to them."

The phrase "the boys" has now come to mean our little grandsons Josh and Kaleb.

Peter walks away under the trees and soon returns, a wide grin spread over his face.

"They sounded so sweet. I told them Grandpa shaved his beard. Josh said, 'You shaved your beard?' And then I heard him call out to Ruth Anne, 'Mommy! Mommy! Grandpa shaved his beard! Grandpa shaved his beard!'"

I visualize Kirk and Ruth Anne in our house, house-sitting. Josh, at three, his blond head barely reaching the kitchen island, and two-year-old Kaleb running about.

"What did Kaleb say?"

"Kaleb? He said, 'Pappa! Pappa!'"

I smile at Peter's delight—my delight.

Softly and with a faraway look he adds, "I told them both that I love them very much."

"Yes, of course."

And now I wonder why I didn't go along to make the phone call. It's as if I wasn't meant to go.

When it's time to tuck in, I realize it's been another extraordinary day.

9

The End of the Road

There is no hurry this morning, as Terry had said to come to the community centre at 11 o'clock when we could join him in the hour of singing he leads at the school. We relax and leave around ten. Terry said it's easy to find the community; there will be a little sign after the *bitumen* turns red.

We drive through Alice, over the dry Todd River, chatting happily, and proceed along the lonely red country road. Mulga shrubs, with contorted thirsty limbs, look like comical dancers. A white gum tree gleams in the sun. The ever-present cloven mountain range echoes the bright blush of the soil. We're wrapped in colour—no wonder they refer to this part of the country as the *Red Centre*.

"So where are we?" Peter asks.

"I haven't got a clue—haven't seen any signs yet."

"Well, has the *bitumen* turned red?"

"I've no idea."

We now more seriously look for the community's name sign. It doesn't appear.

"We've gone too far, I think," I finally say.

"Well, we don't know how many kilometres it is, so let's just drive on."

The mountain still runs parallel alongside but closes in.

Finally, the road gives way to a sandy trail.

"This looks like the end of the road," I say.

Peter doesn't comment but proceeds, slowly, on the soft sand.

The mountain is like a red giant whose bare flanks loom closer and closer. Still, Peter drives on–determined. The giant wins. We come to its sunburned body sprawled out in front of us like a mammoth animal firmly plunked on top of the sand. It completely blocks our way. *That's it, folks, this far and no further.*

"This definitely is the end of the road," I softly say.

"Yeah, I guess," Peter answers sheepishly.

We slide out of the car. The doors click shut.

Dead silence. Not even a bird.

A little overwhelmed, we let our eyes glide over what surrounds us. The massive mountain stretches out in front and to our left, eroded chunks of it strewn to the right. It's all around. It towers over us, dwarfs us, threatens us. We feel small and vulnerable, as if we're in the presence of something great and awesome. It seems to breathe the heavy ghost-like silence. No wonder the Aborigines consider the landscape sacred, formed by creatures long ago. Each hallowed place has a tale.

We walk on the fine paprika sand up close to the rock. Its convoluted surface is grainy, like sandpaper. Wind and sand have carved out a perfect hollow at our feet. It looks like the arch of a colossal foot. We could snuggle in this shallow dome. It baffles me that I'm afraid the rock might crush us.

Peter sighs.

Hushed, we walk back to the car. He starts the engine, follows the ruts left by other travellers; they lead us in a loop around a house-sized burned sienna boulder, back onto the trail. We slowly retrace our steps. The happy bantering has stopped. We've no idea where we are, except there is only one road, so we can't really be lost. Finally, we see the small sign pointing the way to Amoonguna. We turn in a long laneway and spot Terry's caravan standing apart with a large shade cloth rigged over it. We don't see anyone.

"Let's go," Peter says. "I'm tired."

But just as we turn back onto the laneway, I notice Terry out of the corner of my eye, waving frantically, guitar slung over his shoulder. He's so sorry we missed the singing. We are too. We share our lunch with him as he tells us about his life in the community.

Children walk past the caravan on their way back to school. Peter hears their laughter and suggests we step outside to meet them. He chats with them, asks about grades and courses. He insists on a photo. Terry takes the last photos on our film, Peter with his arms around the children.

Terry tells us the community is appreciative of visitors. He guides us around, introduces us, and black hands reach out to us with warmth and friendliness. An elderly couple sits squatted around a little fire. The lady is busy sanding small pieces of wood. Several short lengths of coat hanger metal glow in the little fire. The man grasps one of the pieces and shows us how he burns designs on the wooden boomerangs.

Back in town, we're anxious to see the photos of our trip so far. We wait to have them developed at a one-hour place and are delighted with the results. One taken of Peter and me standing in front of Jim's magnificent bougainvillea is especially lovely. We decide to have copies made to send to the children at home. Another hour's wait. The copies turn out too light and I ask the man to redo them. Another wait.

"I'll go to *Woollies* and get some groceries," Peter says.

It's hot. Peter looks tired after our adventure. He's not returning. I walk to the grocery store. *Oh, there he is.*

Back at the campground, we jump into the pool for a swim. Peter pulls himself out rather quickly.

"I'm going to the camper to lie down. Forgot my nitro."

I swim around by myself, lie on my towel a bit. *Must check on him.* I go to the camper and find him sleeping. *He's doing so well. This is the first day he's mentioned having to take his nitro.* I shower and slip into a comfy cotton outfit. It's 6 o'clock. I decide to lie down for awhile, carefully climb over Peter so as not to disturb him, and curl up on my spot by the window.

Midnight

I wake. Peter is sleeping soundly. I listen to his even breathing.

We didn't even have supper. I'm still dressed—can't be bothered to change now.

I turn over and go back to sleep.

Part II

Angels in the Desert

*"For he will command his angels
concerning you to guard you
in all your ways"*
(Psalm 91:11).

1

Day One

Early dawn light filters softly through the camper's screen. I hear Peter fumble for an ice cube in our cooler. The cooler lid needs an extra push to close and we keep forgetting. I wait for the cooler lid to click shut.

"It didn't shut."

"Right." Peter crosses the tent floor back to the cooler and gives the lid a good slam. He crawls back into bed. I look at my watch: 6 o'clock. I've slept twelve hours!

"Had a bad night," Peter says, sitting up, pillow propped against the tent pole.

"Really?" I usually wake up whenever Peter is up during the night.

"Had so much pain; I think I have the flu. Had to go to the bathroom all the time. Took a shower just now."

I wonder again how it is I didn't hear him. I see him take a nitro pill.

His angina pain is often worse in the evening and in the morning. The doctors say it's because the heart has to adjust to a different position. We've had a hundred mornings like this. Our conversation usually runs along the same lines; in fact, it has become so familiar it sounds as if we're repeating them. Peter informs me of the pain; I offer to take him to the hospital, he refuses, he asks if I'll nurse him, I reassure him, he starts to joke, the pain subsides, and we go on with our day.

I now say my line: "Hon, if you feel that badly, let me drive you to the hospital."

No answer. He isn't saying his lines; no, he's merely skipping to the next line.

"Are you going to look after me? Bring me water for my pills and juice for my Questran?"

My line is: "Yes, Hon, I'll wheel you around in a wheelchair; I'll bathe you; I'll even cut your toenails." But I also don't want to say my line–much less think of the words.

Peter is right on track and turns to humour. He repeats a funny personal story and we burst out laughing. I extend the joke and laughter fills the camper.

"It's too early to get up," I say. "Let's relax a bit more."

I turn over to doze off again. Thoughts fight to be recognized: *We'd better spend another day in Alice and not venture out to Ayers Rock as we've planned to do today. I'd better not say this, as Peter will argue that there's no reason not to go.*

I sense a shiver pass through Peter's body and turn with a start.

"Hon, are you all right?"

No response.

Shocked, I jump up, climb over him, stand beside him, and ask again if he's all right.

No response.

What do I do? What must I do?

I dash out the tent *(I'm dressed!)* and run to the closest caravan on our left to ask for help. No response.

I run back. Check on Peter. Still the same.

I race to the caravan on our right. No one responds. Maybe it's unoccupied. Maybe my knocking is too soft–my voice not loud enough. I rush back into our camper. I hear a breath. *Good.*

Frantically dashing back out, I notice a pup tent set up at the back of our camper. It wasn't there last night. Someone there will hear me.

"Please, is someone here? I need help; my husband is ill!."

There's a bulge in the tent, then the whole thing jiggles.

A young man with one leg in his jeans hops out and hop-runs on one bare foot, all the while trying to get on his other pant leg. Then he races away like an athlete.

Back in our camper, I try to prop the pillow so it's more comfortable. I gently stroke his hair. He expels one very long breath.

Then everything is still. Unbelievably still.

My heart races; panic rises.

I hear vehicles squeal to a stop. Two uniformed ladies rush in. One carrying paddles, the other a mouthpiece.

"How long has he been this way?"

"A few minutes."

"Please wait outside."

Dazed, I'm frozen in place.

"*Please,* wait outside," repeats the attendant impatiently. Her voice drifts in and I obey.

I see two ambulances, two more attendants readying a stretcher. Bewildered, I walk to the tree, lean on its sturdy trunk, head cradled on my arms.

Everything in me trembles. Hot tears well up and a desperate cry passes my lips.

Lord, what am I going to do? What am I going to do?

I become aware of a presence beside me. Out of the corner of my eye, I see glistening white.

I turn my head. Through my tears it looks like something starry white. The early sunlight flickers through the trees and glints off a white garment.

Puzzled, I stare. *An angel?*

I blink away the tears and see a man. He's wearing a bright white shirt. The man speaks. His voice is gentle, soft.

"Is it your husband who is ill?"

"Yes." A stifled sob.

"I have come to look after you."

His words slowly sink in, wash over me like soothing oil—*I have come to look after you.* The trembling lessens.

I blink again and observe him. White shirt, dark pants. Kind brown eyes. Dark hair. Dark beard. Smooth skin. *He could pass for Jesus.*

"Come with me; we'll sit in my car." There's a gentle authority in his voice; I can trust him.

He touches my elbow and leads me to an older model white car parked in front of the ambulances. It's covered with red dust. He opens the door for me, lets me slide onto the long grey leather front seat. He walks around, gets in on the other side.

This is a dream; this can't be happening. What is happening? How is Peter?

As if reading my thoughts the man says, "They're taking some time with him. It's important to stabilize the patient before they transport him."

I nod and quietly cry. *This is not happening.*

"Would you like to tell me a little about your husband?"

Yes, please, hear my jumbled words.

Haltingly I recount the facts of Peter's health: heart surgery, angina pain, medication. My…my *"angel"*…listens…nods. He leaves to check on things. When he returns, we continue to talk and he softly says, "If he was that ill, maybe there is not much hope."

I hear the words but refuse their meaning. *Of course, there is hope.*

I turn around to look at the ambulances. One shakes rhythmically. The paddles.

The man sees what I noticed and calmly says, "I'm going to drive to the gate; we can wait there."

The car moves slowly and stops at the gate.

"They should be along shortly now," he reassures me.

We wait. The ambulances aren't coming.

"I'm going to drive you to the hospital," the man says. "At the hospital there will be a *sister* waiting for you at the front door; she'll look after you."

Sister, the Australian term for nurse, sounds comforting.

He turns the car onto Larapinta Drive.

The car radio crackles: "The patient is now in full cardiac arrest."
The man is silent.

Well, of course, there must be another ambulance out there somewhere tending to another person. The message can't be about Peter.

Silently, we drive into town.

At the Hospital

A large rectangular building sits on spacious grounds among tall trees. My "angel" opens the car door for me and walks with me up the long walk to large glass doors. Something white moves behind the glass and as we come close two nurses open the double doors and greet me with kindness and concern.

"Mrs. Fast?" (*They know my name? How do they know my name?*) "Come with us; we'll look after you."

They guide me across a polished floor to a long dark-stained counter.

"First, let's register your husband." An attendant behind the counter asks questions and fills in a form. I'm surprised to find I have Peter's wallet with me. I must have grabbed it along with my purse as I left the camper.

She asks for details. *Must mean he's alive. Of course he is or they wouldn't want to register him.*

One of the nurses invites me to come with her to a waiting room. "Someone will be there to look after you."

The small white room is furnished with a sofa, some chairs and a low table. A young woman gets up to greet me.

"Hello, Angie? I'm Michelle. I'm here to be with you. I'll stay with you until the doctor comes." She reaches out her hand and gives me a hug.

"Come and sit down. Would you like a cup of tea? Some toast?"
"Yes, please."

Michelle steps into a little anteroom. She's young and attractive with clear skin, clear eyes, long, straight brown hair. *Another angel?*

She returns with a tray and pours hot tea from a pot. She hands me a small plate with buttered toast and jam.

She sits down beside me on the sofa. We drink our tea and I munch on the toast.

"Would you like to talk? Tell me what happened?"

She accepts all I say, nods with understanding. I find refuge in her empathy. It's good to cry and talk.

Time stands still. *What is happening?*

Michelle reassures me a doctor will come shortly to tell us of Peter's progress. "Let's make a fresh pot of tea," she suggests.

Finally, a young man steps into the room with a stethoscope around his neck.

"Mrs. Fast?"

He sits on a chair across from us, a sheaf of papers in his hands. He asks about Peter's medical history. He talks—strange accented words cross his lips, float past me.

Michelle helps out and tries to explain the procedures performed. The doctor continues to speak and when I can't take any more I blurt out, "Are you trying to tell me my husband has died?"

Silence. Then, a hesitant "Yes."

He pauses and kindly explains how for the past hour they've tried resuscitation. Peter did not respond to their efforts.

The information doesn't sink in. The air is too thick to absorb the awful truth. His words float past. I reel. *It can't be. It can't be.*

I gulp for air. *What now?*

Michelle hugs me and softly says, "There is nothing you need to do right now, Angie, except sit here and cry. At 8 o'clock Margaret will come on duty. She'll help you with everything that needs to be done."

So it *is* true. I crumple onto the sofa. Michelle's arm is around me. *Just cry. Nothing to do right now. Just cry.*

Farewell

A nurse enters and gently asks, "Would you like to see your husband?"

It takes a moment before the awful meaning of her words sink in. Haltingly, I answer, "Yes."

We walk across the shiny hall and pause at a door. She tells me she'll wait right outside. She opens it, and I gingerly step inside a small white-walled room. The harsh fluorescent lighting is softened by the warmth I feel. I'm not alone.

I walk to the high bed. Stunned into stillness, I stare at his familiar form, so natural, as if he's asleep.

My eyes caress the dear handsome face. I stroke his cheek, his hair. *It can't be.*

Quietly, I try to absorb what this moment means. This moment is ours and somehow I'm not afraid.

But how do I sum up a thirty-year relationship in a moment? This moment...now! With tears streaming down my face, I say my farewells. A long list of *thank yous* tumbles from my lips: how much his life has meant to me; how much his joy, his faith, has influenced me; how special these last three days have been.

"And now you're free," I whisper.

There's a gentle knock. "Are you OK?"

"Yes; it's just so difficult to leave," I sob.

I ask for a pair of scissors to cut a lock. A tiny part to keep with me. *I need to leave; they're waiting for me.*

I walk to the door, back to the bed, back to the door, reach for the door handle. The tearing in my heart is excruciating. Ripping. Into pieces. I realize part of my heart will always remain with Peter.

As I step through the door, I sense the room is now empty behind me. I gently close the door and stagger, dumbfounded, into life before me.

8 a.m.

When I return to the little waiting room, the social worker is there and greets me warmly.

"Hello, Angie, I'm Margaret. I'm here to help you with whatever needs to be done today." I look into her kind, open face.

81

She takes me upstairs to her bright, spacious office. Dappled sunlight streams in through tall windows that look out onto green treetops. As I enter, I also see a poster of a little soft koala bear hopelessly entangled in a shrub. The caption reads: *Relax, I AM in charge.* This angel must know the Shepherd.

First, the telephone calls. Margaret has already left a message at the Reef House in Palm Cove for Jim to call the hospital. Jim has gone home after his night shift, but the hotel will send someone to the house. His phone is still not connected after their move to Palm Cove.

Now the overseas calls. Margaret has difficulty getting an overseas operator. Finally, my home phone rings and Margaret steps back to give me privacy.

Ruth Anne answers. "Mom?" I hear the edge of fear in her voice.

"Yes, it's me."

"What is it, Mom?"

My throat refuses to release the words I have to say.

"Mom? What is it?"

Every nerve in me resists having to deal her this enormous blow.

"It's Dad."

"Dad!"

"He's gone."

A heart-wrenching cry wells up instantly in both of us.

"Oh, Mom."

Margaret moves close, lays her hand on my shoulder, and I draw an amazing amount of comfort from her simple touch. This has to be the most difficult thing I've ever done. I try to stifle my sobs.

Ruth Anne says, "Bruce just walked in the door! He'll pick up the other phone."

I find my voice, tell them both what happened. Tell them people are kind and helpful. I'll be all right and will call back later with more information.

I replace the receiver and take deep breaths.

Margaret gently asks whether I have any plans as to where to go, what to do. I'm in a fog, feel disoriented, overwhelmed.

The day has only just begun.

The koala bear: *Relax, I AM...*

I remember Peter's instructions: cremation, don't rush home. A tremendous weight lifts. *Thanks, Hon.*

But what about the children?

I voice my thoughts as best I can and Margaret helps me sort it out. It would be best to go to Adelaide, to Peter's niece Loretta, as was our plan. Julie's parents also live in Adelaide, so Jim and Julie could fly down. Peter's sister and husband are travelling in the country, but Adelaide is on their itinerary. Hopefully, they can be located. Adelaide is the best plan.

"A family reunion," Peter said.

The phone rings. It's Julie.

"Mom? What is it?" Fear palpitates in her voice. I see her standing all by herself in the phone booth down the street–Dylan in the stroller. She hasn't woken Jim. I need to tell her. My throat constricts again.

"Mom?"

A deep breath: "Julie, it's about Dad. He's had a heart attack. Julie...he's gone."

"Oh, no, no!" Totally distraught, "I'll tell Jim."

My head plunks on the desk. How horrible to have to deal out this sharp, stabbing pain. Margaret comes to stand beside me. She quietly lays her hand on my shoulder.

The phone rings again. It's Jim.

"Mom? What is it?"

He doesn't know but suspects the worst. Once more–the heart-breaking blow.

"Just come back to Cairns immediately, Mom," he says with deep emotion and concern. "I'll look after everything."

"I've thought about that, Jim, but it would only be the three of us. If you and Julie come here, we'd be together with her parents, with Al and Loretta, and maybe we can reach Aunt Tena and Uncle Henry on their tour. Wouldn't that be better?"

"Yes. I see. I'll arrange for our flights and call back, OK?"

The phone keeps ringing; two overseas calls: one from Dave, our eldest, and the other from Joanne, my best friend. These calls are different and mean so much.

Next: try to reach Loretta. Thankfully, she hasn't yet left for work. She's shocked but, yes, of course, I'm most welcome to come to her place.

Margaret hovers like a true angel, moving close when she senses I need the comfort of her presence, moving to the door when she senses I need privacy. She has offered for me to stay the night at her place. She gently guides me through the next steps: make arrangements with the funeral director; make arrangements to have the body shipped to Adelaide; make arrangements to have the car and camper shipped to Adelaide.

There's a knock on the door. Margaret answers it and says to me, "Someone's here to see you."

Terry Medley from the Amoonguna Community walks in, reaches out his hand. "I drove into town this morning and heard the sad news. I'm so sorry."

He seems as shocked as I am. His thoughtfulness is comforting.

Now–how to pack our gear.

"There's no way you're going to the caravan park by yourself," Margaret firmly states. "I'm going with you."

"Peter met Rev. Doug Turnbull at church on Sunday; he'd be willing to help," I offer.

Margaret dials Doug's number and arranges for the three of us to meet at the park at 12:30.

Next: to the funeral director to sign papers. I'm in a daze and sign my name obediently beside little Xs.

Back in the car, I again express my thanks to Margaret.

She smiles warmly. "I'm glad to be able to help."

"You've spent so much time with me. You must have other work to do."

"Angie, my work today is to help you. And if that takes all day, I have all day."

She glances at her watch. "It's 11:30. I think we can get everything done in order for you to catch the 3:40 flight to Adelaide."

She pulls the car to a stop at the travel bureau and accompanies me to buy my airline ticket.

Noon

Back at the hospital, Margaret brings me a sandwich, makes some tea, and then drives me to the caravan park. Doug is there already.

Clothes for the undertaker. We're camping; Peter only has a short-sleeved dress shirt. I find a crumpled tie, a pair of dark blue pants, white tennis socks–it doesn't matter, the bottom half of the casket will be closed.

Casket?

I give Doug our grocery supplies to give away.

A change of clothes for me; our two backpacks to take along with me. Everything else can be stored in the camper. I guide them in folding it up. I'm on autopilot.

The park owner comes with Peter's camera. "I took this into the office, just to keep it safe."

I thank him for his thoughtfulness and put it in Peter's backpack.

Margaret leaves to take the clothes to the undertaker. I drive behind Doug as he guides me to the train station.

A train is waiting on the tracks. Boxcars, flatbed cars–standing very still, reverently still. A train has stopped to help, after all. It will safely transport our stuff.

I pull out my credit card.

"Sorry, ma'am, cash only."

Doug drives me to a bank and I obtain the needed cash.

When Doug drops me off at the hospital, Margaret is waiting for me with soap and towels.

"You have time to take a shower and then I'll take you to the airport."

My tears flow as copiously as the water out of the showerhead.

Margaret calls, "Jim is on the phone."

His phone is connected, finally! I quickly finish the shower, talk to Jim and jot down his number in my address book. He tells me the three of them will fly out and will arrive in Adelaide tomorrow at 6 o'clock. I'm so glad this worked out.

We gather my things, get into Margaret's car and she drives me to the airport. Over the roar of the aircraft engines, I offer my thanks again and again. We hug each other tightly; we promise to keep in touch.

The flight attendant directs me to my seat in the small craft but then, after a short stare, gives me the option to take another more private seat in the back. Does she also know? My tear-crumpled face must tell all. I gratefully accept her offer.

We rise and bank, and Alice suddenly disappears behind the copper mountain range.

A widowed friend told me at one time how important it was to write some kind of eulogy before the end of the "first" day. I've imagined writing a tribute; it would be a masterpiece of beautiful prose. I fumble for pen and paper in my denim purse. Dry-eyed, dreamlike, I write. Only the bare facts flow from my pen.

Adelaide

Loretta, as well as Julie's parents, Marge and Merv Wilson, are waiting at the Adelaide airport. We're strangers, except I met Loretta some twenty years ago back home in Canada. It's an awkward but warm welcome. Marge hands me a little bouquet of flowers.

"We were so much looking forward to meeting Jim's parents," she softly says. "I'm so sorry we're not to meet Peter."

Loretta drives me to her place. I'm in a fog. It's as if I'm on a trip, meeting new people and Peter is back home. I try to piece the story together for Al and Loretta. They listen. They also don't believe it.

Loretta shows me their guest room. I gratefully climb into the double bed, reach for my journal and write *Day One* beside the date.

My entry begins with "*I've lived a lifetime today.*" I write it all down, eight and a half pages—every detail—and, as I do, I begin to see God's loving hand in those details. I wonder about the people who were around me today, assisting me as if they'd been assigned that place for the day. Why did a young man set up his pup tent, in the middle of the night, directly behind our camper when there were so many empty sites? Who was the man in the glistening white shirt? Who was Michelle? She didn't have a uniform on and it was 6:30 in the morning. Why? And Margaret? How was it she had all day to spend with me? I think of what all three said to me: "I have come to look after you; I'm here to be with you." I think of the koala bear poster: *Relax, I AM in charge.*

Twelve hours of deep sleep were given before I needed to face this day. And in some mysterious way, it was arranged that I sleep with my clothes on. All those nightmares—for nothing!

The teary entry ends with: *And here I am, tucked in a nice comfy bed, and I will try to sleep. The day I dreaded so much has dawned and gone. I was carried. I was led through it moment by moment. Thank You, Lord. May it be a reminder to me in the difficult days to come.*

2

Day Two

Wednesday, October 28

I sense my strange surroundings and instantly am wrenched awake, jolted into the present. I bury my face in the pillow. *Oh, no, let this be a dream. It can't be true. He can't be gone.*

There's a soft knock and Loretta pokes her head around the bedroom door. "I've brought you some tea."

She carefully places a tea tray on the nightstand and says, "I've taken the day off work and will be here to be with you." *Those words! Same words. Another angel?*

I thank her gratefully and sit up to sip the tea.

The day looms before me like an insurmountable mountain. I try to focus on the only things I need to do today: wash and sort the clothes and wait for Jim and Julie to arrive at 6 o'clock.

Loretta has prepared breakfast.

"Tell me again what happened."

I start to recount the unbelievable events of yesterday, filling in details, trying to make sense of it. I'm numb, shocked, confused—a kaleidoscope of emotions whirls around and around. I cry, talk, smile, and then tears well up again.

Loretta listens. Her empathy is soothing, as if she's stroking a very sore muscle. I become aware as I talk that the weight on my chest eases somewhat.

Yesterday at the hospital, I arranged to call home this morning–evening for the children in Canada.

A communal "Hi, Mom," greets me.

And then, "We have four phones plugged into all the jacks at your house, so you can talk to us together. Except Wayne's not here."

I picture them in the kitchen, bedrooms, downstairs family room–my raw heart aches; they're so far away; we're not together, holding, sharing. I do my best. I need to tell them every detail, give them a picture of our last three beautiful days in Alice, the peace and joy their dad possessed, his last letter, his last funny words.

"Just like him," they chuckle.

I tell them about the stranger at the campground and the helpfulness of the hospital staff. Then I share Peter's instructions concerning cremation. They stifle sobs. They understand. I reassure them people are kind, I'm being looked after. I'll be OK.

"Mom, someone has provided me with a ticket to fly out to be with you." Bruce's voice.

"Really?"

"I'll be leaving shortly, and I'll be there on Friday. Is there anything you'd like for me to bring?" he asks.

"Can't think of a thing. Just you come, that's all."

I wash and sort the clothes that are in our backpacks. Peter's clothes. The children will want to have some of the colourful T-shirts he bought here. I want to keep the pink one, the one he wore in front of the bougainvillea.

Loretta fixes lunch.

"Tell me about my Uncle Peter," she asks.

I tell her about his life, his sense of humour, his laughter, his pranks. She recounts the few memories she has of him visiting her parents' ranch on the Canadian prairies. Together we look at his life as if studying a photograph, and it's good; we delight in what we see. It's healing. It's heart-wrenching.

"Now, what about a funeral?" she questions.

My head is spinning; she helps me sort it out.

"I'll make some calls while you rest," she says.

She makes an appointment with a funeral director; a friend offers the name of a minister; and with the aid of the police department she tracks down Tena and Henry and finds that they'll be arriving in Adelaide tomorrow.

6 p.m.

Finally, a tearful reunion at the airport. Jim and Julie, carrying baby Dylan, walk toward us. Marge and Merv have also come. Julie's eyes flit from Marge to me. Whom to hug first? But Jim has me in his arms, so she can go and first be embraced by her mom. Dylan smiles sweetly, totally oblivious of the fact he's just lost the best grandpa in the world.

Marge and Merv are house-sitting Merv's mother's home here in Adelaide, and that's where we spend the evening together. When it's bedtime Jim walks me back to Loretta's place—walks with me in this strange, unreal world.

It can't be. I'm on a trip. Peter will be home when I return.

I reach for my journal and write *Day Two* at the top of the page.

3

Day Three

Loretta knocks at 7:40. My head and body feel like lead–after-effects of the sleeping pill Merv slipped me last night.

Jim picks me up at 8:30 to keep the appointment with the funeral director for 9 o'clock. Merv has offered to chauffeur us today.

We spend a gruelling hour at the funeral home. The director laughs, jokes, and asks my opinion of Alice Springs' scenery. He can't spell. Must be those Canadian names.

"How do you spell Ontario?"

"Could you spell that again?"

"And you've decided to cremate the body?"

"My husband's wishes, yes."

"Would that be fair to the family back home?"

My head is spinning.

I try to think it through. Fair to the family? Do I need to let the children decide? I sign the cremation papers but put everything on hold, leaving the funeral director a happy man.

We rush home for a sandwich and I call Ruth Anne to ask her to confer with her brothers.

12:30 p.m.

Merv takes us to meet the minister. My stomach churns. A minister picked out of a hat, as it were. What will we find?

Relax, I AM in charge.

Rev. Graham Nicholls is tall and broad and has the same kind brown eyes as the man in the campground. He grasps our hands and warmly welcomes us into his book-lined study. I sink into one of the leather chairs. He swivels his chair toward us, and as he looks first at me and then at Jim, he quietly says, "Tell me about your husband, your father."

I sense peace in this wood-panelled room. My tension melts as I start to talk. Jim adds his views, his memories. Rev. Nicholls leans toward us, nods, smiles. "Yes, I see. I understand." I get the uncanny feeling he knows Peter, knows his mind, his faith, his feelings so hesitantly expressed.

Before we leave, he prays with us. I feel immensely relieved, blessed. *Thank you, Lord, for this provision.*

Ruth Anne calls back. They'd very much like to have Dad's body shipped home and have a proper funeral together, but no, they realize his wishes for cremation are best. "Except I haven't been able to talk to Wayne," she adds.

"He needs to have a say. I'll wait."

I put the two chickens in the oven, as Loretta asked me to do this morning, and go to sleep. I sleep all afternoon. The chickens burn.

6 p.m.

We pick up Henry and Tena at the airport. I hug Peter's sister warmly, but in our shocked state the unreality continues.

Isn't Australia beautiful? Peter's not here, just now. He'll be along shortly. I hear his laughter. Dead? Can't be. Don't be ridiculous.

I tell my story once more. The telling sharpens reality. Tena's eyes are filled with sorrow, a loving, caring sister struggling with the loss of a fourth brother—too young to die.

It's too overwhelming and I go to my room, engulfed with grief. My heart feels like a tender damaged place and the heavy weight on it is crushing it, breaking it.

The others in the house are talking, laughing now, sharing trip experiences. This is Peter's jolly family reunion he was looking forward to so much. How can they laugh with him absent?

Tearfully, I call Jim.

"Could you walk over for a bit?"

"Of course. I'll be right there."

He comes to the kitchen door, flowers in hand. The screen door is locked. I fumble with the lock, fighting back tears.

"It won't open," I choke.

"Try again; you have to turn it just so."

I jiggle it, try it this way, that way. Hopelessly, I stare through the screen at my son, separated even from this child.

"Keep trying, Mom." His face, contorted with pain and exhaustion, looks as if he's ready to tear out the screen.

Finally, a click; and the lock gives way. The door opens; we sob in each other's arms.

"I picked these for you." He hands me the little bouquet of flowers. For a split second, I see a little boy with an offering of yellow dandelions.

I'm concerned about the children; we're so far away from each other. How are they coping? What do we need to do about the body? If only we were together!

"It's early morning back home; maybe we can reach Wayne right now," Jim suggests and picks up the telephone.

We connect and, even though Wayne already knows all the details, I now personally tell him about his dad's last days, his peaceful death.

"I need to say goodbye to him," he chokes. "I need to see him."

"Yes, of course, I understand. I'll see to it."

The others enter the kitchen, and we sit around the kitchen table. Loretta makes another pot of tea. I try to think: two funerals; fly home immediately. The others reassure me it needn't be my worry tonight. It's late. Go to sleep. With one of Merv's sleeping pills.

I walk to the door with Jim and he hugs me good night.

"Come and stay with us at the Wilsons'," he says. "There is room for you, and then *we* at least can be together."

I decide to go in the morning.

4

Day Four

I wake at 6 o'clock. Weighed down. Lonely. Gut-wrenching sobs. A flood of tears. Reality is sinking in. He's not here. We're having his funeral today.

I ache for the kids. This is so difficult.

When I hear Loretta in the kitchen, I make an effort to dry my tears. Take a deep breath. Heave this heavy brick off my chest.

"I'm walking over to the Wilsons' to be with Jim and Julie." I manage a near-normal voice.

"Sure, I understand. I'll see you later." She gives me a comforting hug.

It's warm outside, the tears running down my cheeks warmer still. It's as if a fountain had gushed open. The street is quiet, no one around this early.

There's also no life yet at the Wilsons' and I wait discreetly on the covered back porch. *How can I stop crying?*

I hear Merv in the kitchen, but he's in his boxer shorts. Better wait some more. Now I hear Marge playing with Dylan, cooing, singing. I hesitate to knock. But Merv has spotted me on the porch and hails me in, boxer shorts and all. He tells me to join Marge and Dylan in the bedroom while he makes tea.

Marge is sitting up in bed, Dylan happily perched on her raised knees.

"Come and sit down." She pats the blanket. "It must be so hard for you."

The tears flow again. Marge cries with me.

"You need to stay here with us, with Jim," she says. "We have room for you. I'll put up a cot."

I gratefully accept. Her graceful, gentle manner touches me. She's another angel sent to help me get through this difficult day, I'm sure. We play with our beautiful grandson, and Merv brings in the tea tray. We only met two days ago and here I am in their bedroom!

The phone rings. It's for Jim. He calls out to me.

"It's Wayne, Mom. You can speak with him."

"Hi, Mom. I've thought about it all day and it's OK not to ship the body back here."

"Are you sure?"

"Yes, it's best all around."

I realize the sacrifice the kids are making. My heart aches, but this is best.

Marge prepares sandwiches for lunch and we're off to the airport to meet Bruce. He's the first one through the gate and strides toward us. It's so good to see him, to have one more child with me.

The boys and I have an hour to share and catch up before the funeral service. Bruce pulls out the things he's brought for me from his backpack.

First, photos of Daniel—a sweet, blond, blue-eyed boy. Peter said he'd see him—another little guy not to know his grandpa.

"Ruth Anne thought you'd like to wear this," says Bruce as he reaches into his pack.

I unroll my "California" dress. A favourite bought on our last trip there. I remember how much Peter liked the long, rose-covered shirt-dress.

"How thoughtful of her!"

Bruce gives me cards and letters and we read them together. A special envelope contains a letter from each one of the children, lonely in their grief.

Oh Mom, it's so hard to realize and understand that Dad is gone for good—never to be touched or seen again. I'm crying so much, I don't know how I'm going to get through this week. It comes in waves like the ocean. When you think it's over you remember something else, or someone says something, or you hug someone else, and it starts all over again. You sounded so strong on the phone at the worst time of your life. How can that be? I'm crying so much I can't see this page. I love you and Dad.

The family is split in half—three in Australia, three in Canada. A kind pastor has visited and has planned a family service for the three at home.

Twelve of us gather in a room at the funeral home to bid Peter farewell. There is a floral arrangement from Peter's siblings back home, a bouquet from Al and Loretta, and the large casket spray Jim and I ordered.

The boys and I stand by the casket, arms clasped around each other. Tearfully we whisper our thoughts.

"Amazing to think of the way his life intertwined with ours."

"How much he impacted us."

"He brought us so much joy."

"And some tears."

The three of us, no doubt, were the easier targets for his teasing.

"He'd love the look—a dress shirt and tie, cotton pants with a tiny hole in the knee, no belt, white sport socks." We giggle as I explain. "I thought the bottom part of the casket would stay closed!"

"He always made us laugh, and even now he does," Bruce croaks through his tears.

The director closes the casket and replaces the spray of roses.

Bev Shea's rich baritone now fills the room: "In the sweet by and by we shall meet on that beautiful shore."

Rev. Graham Nicholls leads us in a simple service. He reads my eulogy, favourite Scriptures. On one of our early dates, we visited an exhibition and had our names engraved on a pendant. Peter instructed the engraver to turn it over and carve Romans 8:28 on the back.

"That will be *our* verse," he said. "In all things God works for the good of those who love him."

Graham reads a poem by Michael Quoist that came with one of the letters:

Some of the family were sobbing: All is finished.
And I was thinking that everything was just beginning.
Yes, he had finished the last rehearsal,
*   but the play is just beginning.*
The years of training were over
*   but the eternal work was about to start.*
He had just been born to life,
The real life,
Life that's going to last
Life eternal.
There are no dead people, Lord,
There are only the living, on earth and beyond.
Death exists, Lord,
But it's nothing but a moment,
A second, a step,
The step from provisional to permanent,
From temporal to eternal.
As in the death of the child the adolescent is born,
*   from the caterpillar emerges a butterfly,*
*   from the grain the full-blown sheath.*
But where are they, Lord, those that I have loved?
Lord, my loved ones are near me,
I know that they live in the spirit.
My eyes can't see them because they have left their bodies
*   for a moment, as one steps out of one's clothing.*

Their souls, deprived of their bodily vesture,
     no longer communicate with me.
But in You, Lord, I hear them calling me,
I see them beckoning to me,
I hear them giving me advice,
For they are now more vividly present.
Before, our bodies touched, but not our souls.
Now I meet them when I meet you.
I receive them when I receive you.
I love them when I love you.
Oh, my loved ones, eternally alive, who live in me,
Help me to learn thoroughly in this short life
     how to live eternally.

Graham reads from Psalm 139, God's promise to hold us when we "rise on the wings of the dawn" and "settle on the far side of the sea."

That means right now, Lord, hold us right now.

Graham speaks to us. He's a *beaut*, an angel indeed. How else could he know Peter so intimately? Know the beat of his heart? Know the depth of his faith? Understand his wry sense of humour— able to joke in the face of death? "It was his faith that enabled him to laugh and live gloriously," he says.

I feel nourished by the genuine, sensitive words of this football-player turned preacher. A stranger sent to give us aid.

We gather at Al and Loretta's for a light lunch. Friends have provided sandwiches, goodies, drinks. It's good to visit, to chat with a semblance of normalcy. I hear the visitors' laughter and remember laughter after we buried one of Peter's brothers. I thought it strange. They say mourners feel a sense of relief that it wasn't their turn this time. I can't laugh.

Al takes me for a stroll around his yard. I haven't noticed the garden. He names the tropical plants, the flowers. I feel as if I'm taking Peter's place. He'd delight in this walk.

When it's time to go, I thank Loretta for her loving hospitality, for all she's done to help. I tell her Marge has invited me to stay at the Wilsons' so I can be with the children.

"Of course, I understand," she says. "And Henry and Tena will enjoy the guest room."

When it's time to retire at the Wilsons', Marge leads me through the dining room to the music room.

"Is this all right?" she softly asks. Frosted French doors open to an interesting little room, housing a bar and an organ, with a narrow cot placed snugly between the two. A book title flashes through my mind: *Wide My World, Narrow My Bed* (Swindoll). A book about singleness. *Bleak my world* is more like it just now. I thank Marge and gratefully sink onto the low cot.

I toss and turn; Merv's sleeping pill has no effect. At midnight, there is a call from my brother in Indonesia; yet I still feel so forsaken. The extended families back home haven't called. Dark thoughts loom to take away the beauty of the day. Maybe writing will help. Without turning on a light and without wearing my glasses, I print with large letters in my journal the events of the day. As I write, the circumstantial frustration of feeling neglected starts to dissolve and bits of thankfulness well up and grow. The treasure of this day, the essence of this day, begins to emerge, shining. This was Peter's funeral. He was so concerned that it not be too difficult for me. The day was stripped of show and ritual, frantic activity and large crowds. Our goodbye to him was private, simple, intimate. It was reverent and full of meaning. God provided the people to make it so. I'm grateful. I'll cherish this day forever.

And Peter would've loved the way *I* was dressed: old scruffy sandals, a red-dust-covered denim purse, contrasted with a fancy dress. I hear his chuckle.

5

Day Five

Marge pokes her head around the French doors at 8 o'clock and asks if I'd like a cup of tea.

Soon Bruce comes in and sits on the end of the cot. Then Jim and Dylan come—all on the little bed. As young lads they used to come and snuggle their warm little bodies against ours in the big bed. It was for their comfort then. Maybe it still is, but I'm finding great comfort in their coming this morning. Now it's baby Dylan who is being cuddled.

It's good to relax here in this spacious, elegant home. It's lavishly furnished, tastefully decorated with the owner's own artwork. Marge has placed the floral arrangements around the white painted hearth in the living room—one on a little table, another in a copper pot. She's pulled the casket spray apart and made several bouquets of the roses. A large dish of rose buds sits on the kitchen table. "Was that OK?" she asked.

It's lovely. It's comforting. Peter loved flowers; nursed straggly geraniums through the winter; couldn't bear to discard anything growing; coaxed ivy to grow around the walls in his classrooms. He set up contests for his pupils to see whose bean plant would grow the tallest.

The car and trailer have arrived. Both are for sale. Several calls have come in. The camper is set up in the backyard for interested buyers to examine. I decide to go into it—only for a moment. Enough. The memory of the scene is so vivid. It's before my eyes all day. What would I have said if I'd known it was his final hour? His last chuckle rings in my ears. Will I also remember that forever?

After an afternoon nap, I reread the cards and letters that Bruce brought and the few cards that have come from friends of the families here. Also Graham's notes, which he thoughtfully passed on to me. Tears come but no crying spells.

Merv barbecues lamb for *tea*.

"Spring lamb on the *barbie*," he says. He seems delighted to be able to wait on us.

After supper, we drive to the beach to see the sunset and Jim's camera is stolen. Added grief.

Back home, we sit around the kitchen table and while Marge pours tea, Merv entertains us with stories from his *road-train* driving days. A road-train, he explains, is a truck pulling a number of trailers. The run from Alice to Darwin was long and monotonous, and the truckers would think up ways to amuse themselves and shock passing motorists.

"One trucker always took his little dog along," Merv says, grinning. "When a car approached, he'd duck down and lift the dog up high, paws on the steering wheel. The car would invariably stop, turn, and approach the truck once more to have another look at the truck-driving dog."

We imagine the stunned looks on the travellers' faces and everyone around the table laughs. A small sound travels up my chest and escapes my lips. It sounds foreign and forbidden. It rises again and escapes more readily. Muscles not used in days contract. I laugh. It feels strange. As Marge pours more tea, Merv walks around the kitchen to tell his tales. The more he tells, the more we laugh. We double over with laughter.

"We were transporting a load of furniture. At lunchtime we unloaded a fancy dining room suite, set it all up by the side of the road, placed fancy dishes on it, and sat down to eat our lunch."

We visualize the scene, the consternation of people in passing vehicles. Everyone laughs. I abandon myself to the laughter.

I'm going to call Merv my "angel of laughter."

6

Day Six

It would be good to attend Graham's church, but I'm far too exhausted. Better sleep a few more hours.

We go to Al and Loretta's, as everyone has been invited to swim in their neighbour's pool. I sit around the pool with new strangers and sense the awkwardness everyone is feeling. No one knows what to say. Do we mention "it"? Should I say something to ease the discomfort? Or do we just visit and act as if nothing happened?

I feel as if I'm marked. I remember Peter telling me about Hester in *The Scarlet Letter* who was labelled with a scarlet A to mark her as an adulterer; I must have a big black **W** on my forehead. It's repulsive. My presence causes discomfort.

The pool's water is ice cold due to a few frosty nights. I force myself into the frigid water to place some distance between myself and the group of uncomfortable strangers. Maybe the water will freeze my body, numb the pain.

Lunch inside is much better. Tena, Loretta and I linger around the table; we talk, speak of things spared me by being here: no big funeral to plan, no long receiving lines to stand through. It was quiet, more intimate, no fuss, maybe even more meaningful. Peter was one to break the code, to do the unusual; this was all so much like him. We chuckle.

And we can have a grand memorial service when we return home. We'll do him proud.

I walk back to the Wilsons' for a nap while Jim and Bruce drive to the Borassa Valley.

We all meet at Sizzler's for supper. Then Merv drives us around town, proud to show off this beautiful city, anxious for me to see the sights. He takes us where their caravan is parked and extols their gypsy lifestyle. He and Marge rented out their home to travel around Australia in a caravan. He suggests I do the same. It sounds appealing—but not alone.

Henry and Tena left this afternoon to rejoin their tour. Jim and Julie will fly home first thing in the morning. It seems best to take my things back to Loretta's and sleep in her guest room the two remaining nights. Now Bruce can sleep on the cot in the music room instead of in the camper.

7

Day Seven

Bruce arrives at Al and Loretta's after they've left for work. He makes breakfast for the two of us and we take the tram downtown. Bruce knows the city. He travelled here last year and is a confident guide. He points out buildings to me. I have no interest in them.

At Qantas Airlines, I buy a ticket to take the morning flight back to Cairns; my return ticket to Canada is changed to November 12. They give Bruce a seat on the same plane! They waive all restrictions concerning prior notice and they give me a 30 percent discount I am not eligible for!

We wait for them to make all these changes.

"Let's find a quiet spot to have a sandwich," Bruce suggests.

It's the first day I feel somewhat relaxed and it's good to talk together about all that has happened.

After we receive the tickets, we need to deal with the photos. Photos of relatives in coffins are sprinkled throughout Peter's albums. I find it macabre and told him I'd never do that. But circumstances demanded I take some photos for the children at home. We get the roll developed. I hold the package in my hand.

"I think we should go to the Hilton," Bruce suggests. "We'll order tea and cake and in that elegant setting we'll open this envelope."

It works. We congratulate ourselves on how well we handled it.

We buy some gifts and cards for our kind hosts and take the tram back home.

"Anything else, Mom?" Bruce asks.

"There's the suitcase that was in the trailer."

"I'll help with that," he offers.

Quickly, matter-of-factly, he helps me sort through the rest of Peter's clothes: some for him, some for me, some to divvy up, the rest to discard.

"There, done." He snaps the suitcase shut.

After *tea*, we take a brisk walk (the temperature has dropped to 20 C) back to Marge and Merv's to have a final cup of tea. We sit around the kitchen table once more and loathe leaving. After our few days together, they probably know more about us than long-time friends do at home.

Someone bought the camper. Jim decided to keep the Toyota and Bruce, afflicted with incurable wanderlust, has offered to drive it back to Cairns.

"But not through the desert," I say.

"No worries, Mom."

Bruce will come by and take me to the airport in the morning, but Marge insists she'll also come. We don't have to say goodbye tonight.

Tucked in at Loretta's, I note in my journal that this was Day Seven. It's been an unbelievable week. I'm overwhelmed by all the events, the grief, the future. Yet, God provided. Particular people were "there" to help me—sent, as it were, to give me aid: the man at the campground with the kind brown eyes, Michelle and Margaret at the hospital, Loretta, Rev. Nicholls and Marge and Merv. That's seven. There were others, but these seven were special during this past week. I can't help but think of them as "angels." God sent me seven angels for seven days!

8

The Storm

Tuesday, November 3

I'm back in Alice Springs where a week ago life changed in an instant, altered forever. The sun is still shining; the red roads still wind their way into the lonely scrubby countryside; the topsy-turvy Todd still runs dry. The MacDonnell Ranges still rise to cradle this pretty town and I don't have any qualms about being back. It's OK. And it's only for a few hours. I'll sit quietly on this bench in the airport waiting room and time will pass.

Marge and Bruce saw me off in Adelaide this morning. I dreaded the goodbye. First time to be alone, to be on my own. Marge saw my struggle, excused herself for a moment and came back with a bunch of carnations wrapped in cellophane. I had carried a rose around all day yesterday and this morning hastily pulled a carnation out of Loretta's bouquet to take with me.

When I boarded, the stewardess obviously saw my tear-streaked face.

"There are three empty seats in the back. Would you like to sit there?" She bent down to whisper this. It started to rain. I leaned my teary face against the blurred window. It was like in the movies—rain showers when something sad or horrible happens. It feels as if it's all a movie anyway. I'm acting, going through the motions. Still exhausted, I drifted off to sleep.

Now, after a two-hour wait in the Alice Air Terminal, I board the flight to Cairns and sit beside two girls from New York. We chat. I arrange my face into a smile. We brightly share our travel experiences. I catch myself saying "we" and concentrate to say "I."

The plane banks sharply as it descends into Cairns airport.

Jim walks toward me, Dylan slung on his hip, and I dissolve into tears. Six weeks ago, such a happy, joyful reunion and now this. We get into the car. The tears won't stop. The closer we get to Palm Cove, the worse it gets. A flood of feelings. Being back in places where we were together ignites a deeper grief, a grief related to memory. Each memory brings with it searing pain. Hadn't expected the pain to be this severe.

A gut-wrenching sob escapes as I walk into the bedroom Peter and I shared and see a single mattress on the floor, neatly made up, lovingly provided but a cruel reminder.

"I'm sorry," Julie whispers, "The double mattress belonged to the camper."

It's windy. Jim says there's been a storm.

I decide to go for a walk to the beach—may as well tackle another first. Memories crowd and jostle as I walk along the familiar streets. Tears stream. We held hands, we laughed and talked, stole a kiss. I pass the Tea House—can't go in there today. Maybe I'll never be able to go there again.

I stare in disbelief at the ravaged beach. The white sand littered with dead palm branches, pieces of wood, debris. Everything looks askew. It's a mess. A fierce wind still blows off the water. The ocean heaves murky brown waves. They crash at my feet. I sidestep their menacing foaming advances.

Yes, ocean, be angry. Spew out your foam—rage against death and destruction.

I let the wind blow full in my face, toss my hair, sweep my tears. Nature has joined in my storm. It's an odd kind of comfort.

I take a different route home. Tomorrow I'll tackle another section. The journey down memory lane is going to be a long and painful one.

Lord, do you have any more angels?

Wednesday, November 4

Julie and I spend some pleasant hours going into town to pick up Bruce's changed airline ticket. We window shop and talk; I enjoy her company. I'm quieter today, feel more rested.

Later, I walk back to the beach. The wind has died; it's calm. The debris has been cleared away; rows of little waves run onto the white sand. The sea shimmers blue under the sun. Yesterday's fury is spent. It's good to be here, to see this place restored to its previous serenity.

In the distance, a lone blue sailboat gently sways on the waves.

Thursday, November 5

A restless, troubling night as I reach for understanding and reconciliation of my last several years. It's early morning, and everyone is asleep. I slip out to the backyard with Alan Paton's *Instrument of Thy Peace,* the third book Peter found in the mobile library. It wasn't returned. He read sentences of it to me, asked me to read it. I didn't.

Paton wrote the book while his wife was dying of emphysema. He was at a place of surrender. I was far from that. Paton was open, tender, trusting, and learned precious lessons through the pain. I resented the pain. I often feared closeness to Peter would exacerbate the pain of losing him; the parting then would be excruciating. I put up a barricade, thinking it would protect me from pain. I distanced myself from God, even somewhat from Peter. There was a hard place—was it anger? Fear cloaked in anger? At some level, I realized that by closing myself off, I also closed off avenues through which grace, love and blessings could flow. This holiday, these six weeks, and especially our last three days together in Alice, were God's gracious gift so that we could part, tender, trusting, with our love intact.

I'll be mourning not only the loss of what I had but also the loss of what I may have had. I cry out to God, to Peter, for forgiveness. Paton quotes Paul Tillich in *The Shaking of the Foundations*: "But sometimes it happens that we receive the power to say 'yes' to ourselves, that peace enters into us and makes us whole, that self-hate and self-contempt disappear, and that our self is reunited with itself. Then we can say that grace has come upon us."

I thank God for a renewed sense of His grace—grace that comes when we have room to receive it.

Julie comes outside, holding Dylan on her hip with one hand and a platter of fruit with the other. She's arranged it festively with blossoms among the slices and there's a love note from Dylan. Grace.

After lunch and a nap, I visit the Tea House. Get another "first" over with. I sit very quietly, hidden among the plants. Many an afternoon Peter said, "I'll meet you at the Tea House." *He'll be along shortly…*

I find the courage to go to the large guest book lying open on a pedestal and find Peter's entry on September 29th. He signed our names and wrote, "Loved your place." I gingerly take the pen and write: "Angie Fast again—alone." Maybe if I write it, I'll believe it.

I walk to the beach. The beautiful scene holds no sting. The raw pain I experienced here two days ago is somehow almost absent. I understand now how the painful jab of memory accompanying every "first" will lessen and even disappear on subsequent visits. How easy to avoid places because of the pain it evokes. That would make my world very narrow. And the book title was *Wide My World…*

Friday, November 6

I go for a long walk after supper. The emotional cleansing has brought some relief. I'm more relaxed; my steps are a little lighter.

I watch the moon come up over the water. Last month we were here together, snuggled on a blanket under this palm to watch the full moon rise. "Where do you think she'll appear?"

Peter whispered. We sat a long time; it was a lovely night. Then, ever so slowly, as if someone turned on a dimmer switch, soft light appeared far across the dark water. Gradually the glowing bulb became visible, slowly rose and sent a long sheath of shivering light to our feet. I thought of it then as a beam of God's love shining toward us. I think that more so tonight.

Walking back, I feel as if I'm on holidays by myself and everything is all right. It's not sinking in that I'll never see him again. Maybe these days of relaxation and peace are given so I'll be able to face the season of winter back home.

9

"It Was Then I Carried You"

Saturday, November 7

I wake with a horrific heavy feeling. I cower to face another day—alone. The phrase "seven angels for seven days" has been spinning around the last several days. I decide to sit at the Ramada pool and write down all that occurred during the first seven days.

It takes all afternoon. As my pen rolls out the words, I'm astounded again how everything happened, how I was taken care of. I still wonder who the man in the white shirt was who came to the campground. At the hospital, I turned to thank him, but he was gone. I looked down the long sidewalk and thought about the distance. But how could…? It seemed too far for him to have walked it in the short minute it took for me to turn around.

There's so much to write. The pool provides a break when the emotions overwhelm.

At home, Julie asks to read the piece and we talk about death, the losses in our lives.

Jim barbeques chops for *tea*. Then he rakes the yard—he gathers all the wood that the storm brought down in a pile. He lights a match and stands, leaning on his rake, to watch the fire greedily chew the debris. The flames grow bolder, rise higher, curl like ribbons.

The scene sends a shudder through my body—a funeral pyre.

113

The three of us have felt very lonely today waiting for Bruce to arrive.

Sunday, November 8

I wake again feeling weighed down. Can't do this. It helps to read a chapter from Paton, helps to focus on something. Someone. Someone higher.

"Let's have a nice day together," Jim suggests. "After all, we have only four days left. What would you like to do?"

"Attend the service at Trinity Beach where Dad and I attended."

"And then we'll drive up to Kuranda," he adds.

It's strange to tell the other worshippers that the grey-haired gentleman, my husband, whom they all met, is now dead. They find it stranger still. I see them struggle to accept this fact. I can't accept it either.

After the service, we drive up into the hills to Kuranda and browse through the popular Sunday market. I see the T-shirt booth where Peter bought a shirt for Josh with the lettering *Grandpa's little fishing mate.*

On the way back, we stop at Kewarra to look at lot sites and new homes as Jim and Julie hope to build.

"You could buy one also, Mom," Jim suggests. "It would be a great investment!" We continue our "good day" by opening a bottle of port and sitting down to watch *The Mikado.*

At 9 o'clock, Bruce drives in. He tells us about his trip and side trips. It's good to have him with us again.

Monday, November 9

It's Jim's day off.

"Let's all hike up the falls behind Edmonton," he suggests.

Peter talked endlessly about the beauty of the falls when he hiked up with Jim several weeks ago.

"I found a different way to climb up," Jim says. "This way is shorter."

We're a happy troupe, climbing, talking, laughing. Jim, carrying Dylan, leads the way, points out things of note in the mountainside forest, and warns us not to trip over roots and rocks on the damp forest path. I slip and someone offers a helping hand.

Soon we hear water rush and surge and finally, in a clearing, the falls come into view—a long series of cascades splashing down from rocky outcroppings on the mountain. For a moment we stand in awe as we take in the scene. The rock layers are overgrown with green vines and broadleaf plants that cling tenaciously to crevices in the side of the mountain. The burbling stream of water hurriedly finds its way between rock and plant and gracefully spills from level to level like bits of a flowing bridal veil.

"This was well worth the climb," I softly say.

At the bottom of each drop in the falls, a pool of water sits in a carved-out saucer. We wade into one and let the streaming spray sprinkle us like rain. We splash and squeal as Dylan does when Jim swishes his chubby legs through the water.

"Is that the rock Dad sat on when you photographed him?"

"That's the one," Jim answers. "Climb up and I'll take a photo of you."

I crawl up and sit very still on a large round boulder, arms clasped around my knees. On one side is the mountain with the greenery and splashes of water. Through a narrow swath in the trees on the other side, I glimpse the valley below, a wedge of Cairns and the ocean beyond.

"I'm staying up here," I call down.

"We'll throw up a sandwich for you, Mom. Catch."

I catch one but miss the second and it sails back down.

"Come on, Mom," they laugh.

Are we hiding our sorrow, or is it natural to put it aside and just enjoy what is at hand? Is our fun somewhat forced?

I brush away a tear and hug my legs. Peter sat here. On this very spot. I hear his chuckle, his admiration of this magnificent view; I sense his thankful, joyful spirit. Jim told me when he and Peter had reached this spot, they started to sing "How Great Thou Art." They sang and sang—kept on singing—"When I look down from lofty mountain grandeur, And hear the brook, and feel the gentle breeze…."

Tuesday, November 10
4 a.m.

It's been two weeks. The crushing weight still lies on my chest; my heart may rupture underneath this load. I take deep breaths, expand my lungs, try to heave off the heaviness. How am I going to survive? Get through this day? Another week? A month? A year…?

I reach for my notebook. The piece I wrote needs editing. May as well let my tears offer up words.

8 a.m.

I find Bruce in the living room, teary eyed.

"Do you know what day it is?" he croaks.

"Yes, it's two weeks today." Fresh tears well up.

We talk and cry. It's all too much and I return to my room. The pain of his absence claws and tears at me. Only two weeks. How can I march through the rest of my life with this horrendous pain in my chest? Will it ease? When? I'll always miss him. How can the ache of it lessen?

I go for a swim and edit my writing some more. What started out to be therapeutic now feels like added stress, but Jim offered to type it tonight at work so I want it completed.

After lunch, Bruce suggests we drive into Cairns. The change of scenery is good for both of us. I watch the shoppers go in and out of the shops; they chat, laugh, and sit to have a drink at a sidewalk café. I feel strangely out of place among these happy people going on with their lives. I want to ask them, "Don't you know he died?"

"Is there anything else, Mom?" Bruce asks.

"I want to look for a sheepskin. Dad said he'd buy one."

We find the shop and I caress the soft white fur with its kinky waves, select the best one and make my purchase.

I need to close our bank account and there are a few more souvenirs to buy. We're getting ready to leave. Our aborted holiday—our trip of a lifetime—over.

Wednesday, November 11

Armistice Day—the day we remember the war dead. The dead! As if we could forget.

We have one more day together and Jim announces, "I have two tickets to take the new hovercraft to Port Douglas. Let's split the fun."

Bruce and I will board the huge craft in Cairns and Jim, Julie and Dylan will drive up to Port Douglas after Jim has slept. There we'll exchange. Jim and Julie will enjoy the return boat trip while we take Dylan back with us in the car.

We're treated to wine and snacks at the boat terminal. Then, with engines roaring, we glide over the shimmering sea; thin pages of water flare out on each side of the craft. We look like a giant white-winged kite, sailing.

"It's one day at a time, Mom," Bruce encourages me as we enjoy the lunch on board. "And today we're taking a boat ride to Port Douglas."

We explore the tiny coastal town some miles north of Cairns, its vast expanse of white beach, the just-opened grand new hotel. We're ushered into the marble lobby and invited to look around and feast our eyes. Fountains splash, brass gleams, marble floors mirror our shoes and legs.

Several swimming pools surrounded by tables with green umbrellas are part of the grounds. The water looks so inviting, but I don't have my *bathers*. I can't resist and gently lower myself into the water—like a body sinking.

The dryers in the elaborate change room help to dry my dress.

Our last evening together. Jim and Julie bring fish and chips from town. I wrap the gifts and souvenirs and pack most of my things.

Thursday, November 12

The day Bruce and I will fly home to Canada.

Jim told us he could show us the Reef House this morning after his shift. I hear Bruce leave and quickly follow to take my last walk to the beach. Serenity. The long crescent of sand, Double Island offshore, the water—a silky aquamarine, perfectly calm, glistening in the early morning sun.

Peter usually spent this morning hour at the beach. He was so keen to see each sunrise. He'd urgently wake me at 6 o'clock with "If you want to see it, come now!" We'd walk here, sit on the soft white sand, and watch an ever-changing fanfare of colour stretched like flags across the sky. Purples, reds, smudged with orange, turning gold, until a crescent of the fiery ball would emerge out of the water, slowly swell, turn silver and chase the flimsy flags away. Most mornings Peter took the walk alone to watch the splendour. Jim would step out of the Reef House to enjoy the sunrise with his dad. They'd walk home together for breakfast and almost in unison announce: "It was spectacular! Too bad, you missed it—again!" It seemed to me Peter was counting sunrises.

We came down to the beach one morning a few weeks ago…the memory is so clear, so poignantly clear, every detail, his voice, his facial expression, the exact words, the exact spot where he stood…

We walked along the water and I said, "I want to take a photo of our footprints in the sand."

"Why?"

"Just because."

We walked together—wet sand squishing between our toes. We stopped and I snapped some pictures. Two sets of prints, one broad and large, pointing out; mine, smaller and straight. Grey blobs of cloud edged with pink, the pink reflected in the water.

"I want to take a photo of just mine."

"Why?"

"I just want to."

I waited until a gentle wave erased our prints, so gently and so carefully washing away all traces of the previous moments. Then I walked alone, looked back, clicked the shutter.

"Child, where you see one set of prints, it was then I carried you."

I find Jim and Bruce at the Reef House in a happy mood.

"Your story is done," Jim says. With a grin he adds, "And the sunrise was beautiful. Too bad you missed it–again."

"It's OK. I have memories."

"I'll give you a grand tour," he continues, and we admire the hotel's white-shuttered rooms, dining areas, and the huge waterfall that cascades down into a swimming pool like a miniature Niagara.

The boys have come up with 101 ideas to keep me here.

"I need to go home."

"Yes, of course, Mom; just dreaming."

"I'll be back," I say.

We're desperate to squeeze every drop of time out of the hours we have left together today. We try to talk, share, but a deep sadness has lodged in all the spaces between us and hampers conversation. We don't want to part. To leave Jim and Julie here to grieve alone seems so cruel. To go home means to face a stark reality.

We leave for Cairns at 3 o'clock, sit by the water at the Esplanade, drink champagne with our pizza, and bravely try to be cheerful while fighting back our tears. Our flight leaves at 6 o'clock. The goodbye is wrenching. We need to go and after still another hug, Bruce and I board the aircraft.

High over the Pacific, with four seats available to stretch out on, sleep escapes me. Ideas flood my mind for the memorial service we'll have back home. We'll celebrate his life! His life as he lived it at home, at school, in church. Songs to sing: "Take Thou My Hand, O Father." We sang it often when I was a child in war-torn Holland. Claudia, Peter's favourite soloist, will sing "Love One Another." John and Lottie will sing "One Day at a Time." It all fits together–

as if it were already planned. I rummage in my bag for a piece of paper to jot down some notes.

"You OK, Mom?" Bruce asks sleepily, lifting his head off his pillow.

"Yes, I'm OK." I whisper. "Go back to sleep."

Part III

Springs in the Desert

*"I am making a way in the desert and
streams in the wasteland"*
(Isaiah 43:19).

Part Three

Springs in the Desert

1

November

Vancouver is cold and rainy when we land. It's still only evening, still the same date as when we left Australia some fourteen hours ago. Peter said, "Imagine, we get a whole extra day when we return." Hmm! The last thing I need is an additional day!

I slosh through the rain, feet freezing in my light canvas shoes, on our way to an upscale hotel (Bruce's trick to soften the hardships of travel). I sink into a plush red curved seat and after tea curl up to rest, hidden behind a generous red tablecloth. We have a seven-hour wait.

Sleep finally comes on the night flight from Vancouver to Toronto.

Friday, November 13

When we arrive in Toronto, it's morning. Diane and baby Daniel, as well as David and Carol, are waiting to meet us. It's an anguished reunion, but for the moment, our focus is on life given rather than life taken. Seeing baby Daniel dulls the knife-edge pain of Peter's absence just now. "I *will* see him," he said. *I'm seeing him, Hon, and he's beautiful!*

123

During the drive home, I'm chatty. It's not real.

We turn onto the driveway. I climb the veranda steps. This is difficult. Dave opens the door for me. I'm home. The house is full. The rest of the children are here; Josh and Kaleb run to me, but everything shrieks his absence. A vague sense of wrongness inhabits the place; even the clock's tick is tinny and cold. I walk into our bedroom to set my suitcases down and reality strikes like lightning. I gasp for air—shrink back and quickly leave the room, stifling an overwhelming sob.

Joy and sorrow sit together today, inseparable. We're so very glad to finally see each other again, yet the sadness is so profound. We spend the day catching up. What happened in Australia; what happened here at home. The children share with me the service they had, the concerned kindness of family and friends. They show the photos they took—pictures of all of them strolling in the fallen leaves. It was spring in Australia, but as I see the children framed in autumn colour, it strikes me that it was fall when he fell.

"Mom, we've found Dad's prayer diary," the children inform me.

"We've been leafing through it. It's touching to see our names."

They give me *My Personal Prayer Diary*—gold letters etched on a brown cover. It's familiar. I gave it to Peter eight years ago as a Christmas gift. He asked for it. I've never opened it. It was private. I hesitate to open it now. It's a daybook compiled and written by Catherine Marshall and her husband, Leonard LeSourd. Each page contains a Scripture verse and a short prayer-meditation. The rest of each page is blank for the reader to use, to record prayers and answers to prayer. I see Peter's scribbles—blue, black, red ink; boxes drawn around sentences, some heavily underlined; notes, prayers, weight records, diet struggles. He's been jotting things down for eight years, cramming notations into the same small spaces. Some pages are blank. I'm not up to looking at it more closely.

The children prepare a turkey dinner with all our favourite trimmings and we gather around the dining room table. Peter always sat in the chair by the windows. It screams his absence.

"I can't sit there," I finally say, sensing the children are waiting for me to sit down. "Maybe next time I can do it," I mumble.

We stand around the table awkwardly–the truth of the vacant chair burning our eyes, burning deep into our being. It's only a chair! How can an empty chair hold such intense power with my emotions?

"You sit in it," Ruth Anne whispers to Dave.

He leads us in regrouping our seats around the table and prays a blessing on our meal. It's Friday the 13th. The first day Peter and I were truly together; the first day I feel so desperately alone.

Sunday, November 15

Sunday morning: tea in bed, Peter singing–off-key–getting dressed for church, breakfast at the bay window…

The children leave to attend a service. I wander around the house as if I'm lost, crying, searching…he's not here–I checked all the rooms. They say Sundays are the worst.

The prayer diary is on the coffee table. I reach for it and curl up on one of the blue rockers by the bay window. The beloved view of our wooded backyard has never failed to soothe, but the reality of his absence, also in the yard, stuns me and all I see is a naked, hollow space. A biting angry wind tears at the last of the leaves. The deck is white with frost. Through a gap in the trees, I can see the fruit orchards next door that we used to own, and a sliver of the red barn that Peter and the boys built after the old one burned to the ground. He brought so much to this place, the farm, this yard, the woods. How can it all continue without him? Tears keep gushing.

The *diary*–I hold the book almost reverently and let the pages fan from my thumb. I'm still hesitant to open it; it wasn't meant to be mine. I find today's date. The passage quoted is Colossians 1:11. "Strengthened with all might, according to His glorious power…." (NKJV).

My raw heart struggles to grasp the truth. In the meditation, Peter underlined "Lord, be my strength to endure joyously." He struggled with lack of energy, lack of stamina, angina pain. Yet, he was joyous.

The book suddenly seems like a gift. It could be my companion during the coming year. The words on these pages may guide me on my journey through grief. I may sense Peter's nearness as I read what he wrote—learn from him, touch his soul, the essence of his spirit. Maybe the book *was* meant to be mine—a precious gift.

I turn to yesterday's page. Peter's prayer jolts me: *May You be to her a Comfort, a Shepherd—may You be to her Wisdom. May she find a Balm for her hurt.*

He prayed this for *me* last year, yet I find it today!

His heart. He was slow to show his heart. Yet *now* I know: *Be to her a Comfort, a Shepherd, Wisdom, a Balm for her hurt.*

The hurt today is so great (no comparison to the hurt that prompted these words), the truth contained in the prayer so needful. With God there is no time. He may well have moved Peter to write these words last year in order for them to drop into my need today. I'm not left to flounder, struggle alone. It's as if another angel has been sent to help me.

Later

I walk around the block. Someone asks, "Alone?"

Yes, don't you know he's gone?

Monday, November 16

Hassles at the bank. "Sorry, Mrs. Fast, your joint account is frozen for ten days."

"I've had this account for thirty years; I need money today; it's in my name."

"Sorry, bank policy."

I glance at the next teller. She knows me but is busy with another client and does not look my way. Tears well up.

Hassles at the pharmacy: "Sorry, your doctor did not phone in the prescription."

I drive to the doctor's office. The receptionist seems not interested and uncooperative, claims there was no message and the doctor is busy.

"My husband is dead; I need this now," I spit out angrily.

I'm not myself. I avoid the grocery store, afraid a head may turn the other way. I escape to the lake, sit on the bank by the water and weep. It's not just losing Peter; it's all that comes with it. People shy away because of their discomfort with death. I've become an embarrassment—a reminder of death. The **W** on my forehead is unsightly.

C.S. Lewis in *A Grief Observed* thought that maybe the bereaved should be isolated in special settlements, like lepers. I thought his comment a little far-out when I first read it. Now I understand what he meant.

But the children come for supper and more family and friends drop in tonight. I'm surrounded with love. The house rings with laughter as if we're having a party—they're having a party.

~Prayer Diary:

"So do not fear, for I am with you...I will strengthen you and help you; I will uphold you with my righteous right hand" (Isaiah 41:10).

The timely words sink in, ease the heaviness in my chest. God promises to hold me, to uphold me. Catherine Marshall writes: "I begin to understand that Your way is not to remove my difficulties immediately but to give me adequacy to cope through the strengthening of Your Spirit." She lost a husband; she walked through the valley of grief. Her words bear weight.

Peter's prayer today was written three years ago: *Lord, I pray for all our kids, and I pray that you'll continue to help us all in the family.*

Yesterday he remembered me, today the children! If I never open this book again, the notations of these two days will have sufficed.

Thanks, Hon. Thanks for your heart of love. Every nerve in my body cries out for you.

127

Tuesday, November 17

God knows of my need and someone comes to visit this morning and someone else this afternoon. Both are comforters in the truest sense of the word. They walk with me and I share with them the blessings of the "angels" in Alice. They look forward with me to the memorial service on Saturday.

Saturday, November 21

A photo of Peter, a bouquet of flowers, and a guest book are on a table in the church foyer. People enter, warmly greet me, offer their condolences, sign their names. The large sanctuary fills for the memorial service.

David welcomes everyone. Scriptures are read; prayer is offered.

Wayne reads a short obituary. He comments on how good it is to see so many familiar faces. "It makes me feel proud to see my dad touched so many people's lives."

One of Peter's colleagues tells of Peter's teaching career and his love of children. Claudia sings "Love One Another and Bring Each Other Home."

Bruce shares what he wrote early this morning:

My first son was born
a month before my father died.
One life began—
another ended.
Fatherhood was passed down
from my father to me.
And life goes on.

Dad,
How did you give me this love for life?
I need to know
so I can give it to my son

and share it with others.
Was it something you said?
Did you try to tell me?
Sure you did,
but I did not hear just your words.
It was your life that showed me;
it was the way you lived
that taught me how to live.

And how did you live?
It was quite simple really.
You took the time
to enjoy the life you were given
and you took the time
to bring me and others along.
How else could you have given me
your love of nature?
You brought me along
to watch you enjoy it.
I was often too busy running ahead,
discovering some large oak tree
or hidden cave,
to stay and listen to you name the flowers
or explain what the bees were doing.
But I did see you
admire those trilliums
and noticed the simple joy you had
in growing an ever increasing variety of plants.
I realize now,
though I took little notice of it then,
it was you who taught me
to love and respect nature.

But how did you teach me patience,
to live one day at a time,

to not fear death,
and all those other truths
a father longs to teach his son or daughter?
I can't remember
any time you sat me down
to try to convince me of these truths.
You patiently watched me,
you gave me freedom
to make my own mistakes
and you always believed in me.
You believed
that if you lived your life
the best way you knew how,
I would see and understand.
And you were right.
Whenever I am being stubborn,
I remember how you changed,
how you learned to admit
when you were wrong.
Every time I am proud,
I remember you facing the whole church,
apologizing for the hurt
you may have caused someone.
Every time I am too tired
to give any more,
I remember you giving more
when you had given all you could.
When I think I have all the answers,
I remember you constantly searching
for new truth,
continually working out your faith.

I want so much to tell my son and others
how to enjoy life,
yes, even death.

But it can't be told.
I can only hope that
as others watch me live,
they will see in me
the same I saw in you—
a reflection of the One
Who gives life
and is Life.

Ruth Anne reads her tribute:

During the past week, I've had a chance to look over some old let-
ters Dad had written to me. There was always mention of the lat-
est book he was reading and he usually recommended that I read it
also. He would often discuss a sermon he was working on or a verse
that had special meaning. Always evident was his striving to grow
to walk closer with God and the excitement of that relationship. He
wrote of a cousin who had died while getting dressed for church and
he said, "Imagine expecting to worship in a church and instead wor-
shipping in His very presence."

And then, there was his funny, sometimes sarcastic, sense of
humour as he wrote about a late night Rook game and how he bid
so high in order to bring his secret partner's score down. I would be
able to imagine his tearful laughter.

More personally, there was my own relationship with Dad. "A
rose among four thorns," he would lovingly say. But there's no way
I can express to you how special our relationship was—that will be
mine to cherish.

But I can say this: the special memories of my childhood have
been relived in the past few years as I have watched and savoured
the time that Dad has spent with my two sons, Joshua and Kaleb.

Building the Frosty family in the front yard.

Singing songs as they walked—always patiently teaching, talk-
ing about the birds, the trees, names of different flowers.

Hearing the old familiar school poems like,

131

The golden rod is yellow
The corn is turning brown
The trees in apple orchards
With fruit are bending down (Jackson).
     As Joshua boasts of his fishing trip with Grampa and as I
remember the look on Dad's face when he was present at Kaleb's
birth, I am so very, very thankful that this same gentle, loving man
who once gave me donkey rides on his knee had the chance to con-
tinue to bring laughter and joy to yet another generation.

Ruth Anne also reads my tribute—a glimpse of our life, our last days in Australia, his last talk to the Aborigine children in Alice. I hope my words will bridge a gap, fill in the missing pieces for our friends and family here, provide some closure. It ends with:

Peter, you so often felt the limitations and imprisonment of a sick
body. You longed to experience yet another dimension of freedom. We
mourn your passing and will miss you so, but we rejoice with you
in your new-found freedom.

David's tribute is in the form of a letter:

Dad, this is the last letter I'll be writing you. You won't be able to
read it, but I hope you'll hear it and understand.
     Dad, I'd like to thank you for so much.
     First, as a child, waiting expectantly by the dining room win-
dow, I'd like to thank you for the security I had in knowing you'd
return from work every day as you promised.
     For the patience I learned early in life, having to wait for meal-
time devotions to be over before I could leave the table.
     I'd like to thank you for the discipline I learned in the many
trips we took to the woodshed, after I overstepped those unwritten
boundaries of behaviour.
     For the many happy times we spent together: those Saturday
afternoons on the toboggan hills of Niagara, those Saturday evenings
watching hockey on TV, eating popcorn. And those long summer
trips across Canada when we would sit together in the front seat,

following our progress on the map like two lone adventurers in the middle of the night, while everyone else was sleeping in the back of the station wagon.

Secondly, as a boy, I'd like to thank you for the friendliness you showed to any and all of the neighbourhood kids, which made our house the focal point of those never-ending games of hide-and-seek, and for showing me how to share love with kids who needed another father or the love of a father they never had.

I'd like to thank you for the personal freedom you gave me to explore my rapidly expanding world and for the continued discipline I experienced—unlike the woodshed variety—when I abused that freedom.

I'd like to thank you for showing me the advantages of an even-tempered nature when you hardly expressed any frustration with mechanical failures or any anger with major disasters on the farm. And, for showing me the importance of humour and laughter, expressed most vividly during our family Rook games when you would leave yourself breathless and in pain because you laughed so hard.

I'd like to thank you for illustrating the importance of worship and the impact of God in your life through the countless hours you spent studying in your chair for Sunday school lessons or the occasional sermon and by allowing me to catch you kneeling by your bed in prayer.

Finally, as a man, I'd like to thank you for making us aware of your health condition little by little, which up until this time didn't seem to be an issue at all.

And, looking back over my childhood, I'd like to thank you for the ways you spent time with us despite your health. You couldn't race us on our bicycles, but you did ride with us and followed at your own speed. You couldn't play our running games, but you would go for walks with us—the most memorable being along the Bruce Trail during autumn.

I'd like to thank you for the example as a husband, always striving to be more loving and always accepting counsel to curb your

133

natural joking approach to communication, which sometimes left others feeling that you weren't as sincere as you really were. And, for showing me that the roles of husband and wife are not defined for a lifetime, when I would arrive home on weekends and invariably see you doing the dishes or stewing up your own version of borscht on the stove.

I'd like to thank you for showing me the kind of attitude toward life that doesn't let one give up living and the kind of lifestyle that is full, yet unhurried, made up of big projects and illustrious plans right until the end.

And, Dad, as I'm writing this letter, I realize there are many more things I'm thankful to you for—some I'm still discovering with each new day. For these I'll have to wait until we meet together in that place to thank you again face to face.

I sit very still and realize how healing it is for the children to express themselves, especially so because they missed his death, missed seeing his body, missed the official funeral. The balm of all their words fills my heart. Their words also enter other hearts. Later someone tells me, "There was not a dry eye in the audience."

After our tributes John sings "There'll be light in the sky from the palace on high, when I come to the end of the road." Not the impenetrable mountain barrier but "a gate open wide."

Carol reads Rev. Nicholls' meditation given at the funeral in Adelaide—my attempt to bring what happened there home to our loved ones here. John and Lottie sing my prayer: "One day at a time, sweet Jesus, that's all I'm asking of you." Pastor Jack thoughtfully pulls all the threads together in his closing remarks and prayer.

My heart is full.

Sunday, November 22

I curl up on the La-Z-Boy chair, listen to the memorial service tape, and finally shed the tears stuffed behind my eyelids all day yesterday. Couldn't cry during the service because I was bursting with pride and love for the children—real troopers. What a beautiful memory. We did him proud. Crown him, Lord!

I'm thinking of that last night on Anzac Hill when he asked, "What more do I want?" Was he saying as much as: "It's OK, Lord, I'm ready to go"? I wish now I'd asked him what all he was thinking about. But how could I have been where he was? We were not in step. He told me several times, "The living and the dying are on different paths." I was filled with the joy of life and love that night— he was saying goodbye to life and sunsets. "Goodbye, God be with you, evening October sky." When the sun set, he, not I, was aware that the city lights were turned on. "The City of Light," he said. What were his thoughts? If I'd asked, would he have truthfully answered? I expected him to live. I fully expected us to return home together. Maybe Peter didn't.

Yet, God kept his promise to be with us, to hold us.

I'm remembering all the "I love yous," the walks, holding hands, dropping everything to be with him. I feel I've been most privileged and have had much more than most women hope for.

If I just stay here embraced by his chair, it'll be as if he's still here. But he's not.

I try to nap but am too busy processing it all.

I call Jim and Julie to tell them about the service. I'll send them a tape. Dylan cut two bottom teeth. They bought a lot in Kewarra and are looking for a builder. I can visualize it all.

Monday, November 23

I'm overwhelmed with all that needs to be attended to: pension claims, insurance claims. I'm saddled with bills: ambulance, three funeral directors' services. The ashes haven't arrived as yet. We still need to have a burial; there are thank you notes to write.

Wayne accompanies me to the bank to check the contents of the safety deposit box. The will is not among the papers and coins.

So, Hon, you were so concerned I know where the key was! How come you didn't know the will wasn't even in the box?

Telephone calls come in about work: a request to teach winter term courses, also a new job offer. I feel so fatigued, as if I'm concussed. I'm too exhausted to plunge back into the work world. Hadn't realized grief was so physically demanding.

Leafing through Job, looking for comfort, foraging for food, I find: "What I feared has come upon me; what I dreaded has happened to me. I have no peace, no quietness; I have no rest, but only turmoil" (Job 3:25,26).

~Prayer Diary:
"Enable me to grasp deep in my spirit that there is never lack in You, Lord."

Wednesday, November 25

Night adds an oppressive dimension. I wake around 4 o'clock most mornings and the next moment the strong tentacles of grief grip me again. I feel tense, nervous, shaky, panicky, disoriented. My heart pounds. Grief feels much like fear. I *am* afraid. I fear the void that is so immense, greater than anything that still is. I'm walking through a dark, desolate night.

Ruth Anne drops in, tries to comfort. Everything within me screams that it be not so. My whole being rebels. *It's not fair! I didn't ask for this!* I feel shattered, as if everything in me is ripped apart, torn, crushed.

There's a family birthday party in the evening and I sit through it dazed, silent. I feel detached, as if I'm observing the scene from somewhere else. Everything seems so senseless, so totally lacking in purpose. I wish they'd let me talk about Peter.

There are no notations from Peter in the diary. The verse speaks of the cares of life choking the good seed. I must take heed not to let grief choke what is good.

"I have been allotted months of futility, and nights of misery have been assigned to me. When I lie down I think, 'How long before I get up?' The night drags on, and I toss till dawn" (Job 7:3,4).

Thursday, November 26

Thank God for a better day today. I label file folders and make telephone calls all morning. There will be umpteen forms to fill out.

Wayne drops in at noon. "Hi, Mom. I'll go through Dad's desk once more."

Soon he stands in the kitchen doorway, an impish grin on his face much like his dad's.

"Found it–tucked away between our old report cards." He triumphantly holds up the lawyer's packet.

We laugh. So much like Peter– *"Let's put this away so we won't lose it."* Invariably he'd forget where he placed it. With the will in my hands, a tremendous load lifts.

I place thank you notes in three church bulletins and have a nap.

Paton says a sense of fortitude comes when we do what we believe to be right.

Friday, November 27

One month. Ruth Anne invites me to accompany her to the Festival of Friends craft show where she has a booth. I wait on customers, wander around, buy each child a Christmas gift, and imagine how it would've been with Peter here, picking out the gifts, laughing, going for lunch...

Last month's morning scene hangs before my eyes all day. It's as if someone has pulled down a screen and the images are projected continuously. I'm powerless to turn it off.

Saturday, November 28

The "scene" is not constantly present today. Is it really that strongly associated with the date? When a friend came to visit, she said that it was her "bad day," the 17th anniversary of her husband's death. "It never goes away," she said.

I go out for a cup of coffee, alone–trying on my new role. The sadness is so deep, a bottomless pit of sadness.

Our good friends, Judy and Klaas, invite me for supper. Judy wisely places me in "Peter's chair" around the dining room table. This way we won't be staring at the empty chair all night.

~*Prayer Diary*:
God commands his people to leave some of their harvest grain, their olives and their grapes "for the alien, the fatherless and the widow" (Deuteronomy 24:19-21).

Catherine Marshall asks: "What lonely or needy ones would You have sit at our table?"

Thank You, Lord, that Judy understands your heart.

Sunday, November 29

I attend church—another first. Strange how the place where comfort supposedly is dispensed is today a place of discomfort: too many memories, too many emotions, too many people, too many eyes, glancing, looking, wondering. The weight of all their thoughts presses on me. The truth of Peter's death stands like a wall between us. If we want to be real with each other, we'll have to dismantle it by acknowledging his death, speaking of it. By rights, they need to speak of it first. If they're not comfortable doing so, they'll avert their eyes, turn the other way and avoid me as I've avoided others in the past. It exhausts me to think of the many "first" meetings still to come.

I can't sing. The words stir intense emotions. The shift from singing to crying occurs so easily—same voice, same muscles. Will I ever be able to sing of heaven again?

Leafing through Job, I find him telling his friends: "Now you too have proved to be of no help; you see something dreadful and are afraid" (Job 6:21).

Monday, November 30

I accompany Ruth Anne to Toronto. We stop to see an acquaintance whose husband died some years ago. I look to her for understanding; she gives advice. I can't absorb it all.

I realize how critical I've become of some of my comforters. I object when someone strokes and shushes me, when someone tells me to just make myself a cup of tea, when someone doesn't call or drops by only to laugh and joke and try to distract me, or when someone says, "Call me if you need me." No one can get it right, because no one can take away the pain. No matter what they say or don't say, the pain remains. Someone wisely told me, "Your friends are saying what they've always said, but you receive it in a different light because your pain is so great."

I need to receive thankfully, whatever they give. I'm glad for the ones who do give what I need most—an accepting, listening ear.

And now another first—alone in the house. Kirk and Ruth Anne have found a house to rent and have moved out today. This is for the best. I have to learn to live alone.

2

December

The cold breath of winter blows; wet snow slants across the yard. I gather wood and fill the woodbox and try to light the fire.

Peter always lit the fireplace. He made such a blaze one year burning the Christmas tree that it resulted in a chimney fire; it sounded like canon balls exploding. He loved the big brush fires made on the farm when tree pruning was finished. And, as if that weren't enough, he made little brush fires in our woodlot. One day he left one unattended. It spread. Jim and a friend came home to see flames greedily lick tree trunks. They frantically stomped it all out, saved the woods.

A blaze of memories...

The fire cheers the room. I'm thankful for my home. Someone said I shouldn't return to it, the memories would be too painful; move somewhere else. I can't imagine doing that. This house seems to wrap its arms around me. I can imagine him to be here still. I can almost hear the squeak of the La-Z-Boy's footrest as he raises it.

Peter was on sick leave when we had the house built. Uncharacteristically he left most of the decisions to me. "It's your house," he'd say. When I hung the ruffled country curtains in the dining room, I turned around from my perch on a chair and saw tears in his eyes. "What is it?" I asked.

"I'm so happy to see you happy," he answered, blinking away the tears. It was not like him to express himself so honestly. Was he thinking I'd be here alone someday? *Alone?*

I want to settle down and read something. My concentration is so limited, my mind so weary, too clouded to see through the fog that surrounds me. The widow said to read the psalms. "Underline every emotion that pertains to you," she said. Sounds like a good plan. I need to focus on something else besides this immense pain. I need bifocals.

"Blessed is the [woman]…[whose] delight is in the law of the LORD" (Psalm 1:1,2).

Saturday, December 5

I've looked forward to a weekend visit in Waterloo with Bruce and Dave and families, but despite the comfort we find in each other, in holding baby Daniel, it's another painful first. Peter is not here and an aching emptiness fills every minute of the day. I walk along the streets, crying, lonely. I try to console myself that next time I won't experience this jab of red-hot memory and it will be easier. I need to experience the pain of all the firsts in order to heal. If I avoid the pain, it will burst open at some future inopportune moment. *Pain does not decompose when we bury it.*

I dreamed about him again. In my dream, I was with a group of people who looked to me for answers to questions about Peter. I didn't have the information but suddenly saw Peter standing apart from the group. Smiling, he gave me the answers. No one else saw him or heard him. It was like a spell. I asked him, "Did you know you were going to die?" He looked so peaceful and gave me a smiling answer, which I can't remember. He disappeared and I took an elevator up to my floor. As I emerged, Peter was waiting for me in the hall and, with a knowing grin, handed me a cup of hot tea. I was overwhelmed to realize he knew where I'd be and what I'd need. I exclaimed to someone that this would change my perspective on grief. I would no longer see things only from an earthly point of view but would keep the eternal in mind. The painful would take on new meaning.

I woke—desperate to hang onto the beautiful dream.

Questions whirl; this is new territory. I haven't walked this way before. Is there communication between the physical and the spiritual world? Does he see what is happening here? Ruth Anne told of a discussion she had with him before we left for Australia. They talked about the possibility of him dying and not seeing each other again. Peter said, "I believe I'll still be able to see you." She wondered how he could experience complete happiness in the afterlife while seeing our pain and struggles here. He answered, "Because I'll be seeing it from an eternal perspective."

In the evening, we get together to watch a movie. It's an Australian movie, the kids inform me. "I must warn you, Mom, the husband in the story dies."

With that information, something within me bolts shut. I determine not to cry.

We settle down with a bowl of munchies, and *We of the Never-Never* begins. A husband brings his new wife to live on a cattle station far into the outback. We see their lives unfold with various setbacks and challenges in a harsh environment. We see him suffering a heart attack. We see her grief. The children glance my way from time to time, but I have determined not to cry. The movie ends.

Wanting to keep the tight lid on my emotions, I head for the kitchen and mutter, "I'm heating some milk and going to bed."

Sunday, December 6

I meet Dave downtown for a cup of coffee before I drive back home. We talk about the movie, the tearless viewing of it. He knows me as an emotional person. My tears are easily triggered. He expresses his concern—not shedding tears.

"I shed volumes of tears," I explain.

During the drive home, I turn it all over in my mind. I sense again how much we missed not being together as a family in

Australia, not sharing the experience of Peter's death, not sharing our tears. Maybe they chose the movie as an attempt to replay the events, a vehicle to bring what happened in Australia closer to home. Maybe they needed this time to cry with me, permission to cry together.

Dave and I talked about the difference between losing a father and losing a husband. I was their age when I lost *my* father. My grieving Peter is such a private affair. There's a strange comfort in that. In private I remember him, cry for him.

It is said that a private love demands a private grief.

But the children—have they been eclipsed by the magnitude of my own pain? Their grief may be different, but it's as real as mine. It may have been better to just have wept through the movie and let the children weep with me.

How did I accomplish this feat of blocking the fountain of tears? Part of me is still in denial; I still walk around in a fog. A blanket of haze lies over everything. Half of the time I don't believe he's gone. To let myself watch the movie with all my heart—was that too risky? The feelings too overwhelming? The full force of the pain too much to cope with?

We of the Never-Never. The phrase interjects again as I veer onto the Queen Elizabeth Way and something connects. Peter spoke this to me! He said these very words! He watched this movie on the flight to Australia! I woke up just when it was over and asked with consternation, "You stayed awake to watch a movie?"

"It was great," he said. "It was called *We of the Never-Never.* This couple moved into the outback and..." his voice trailed off; he averted his eyes, fumbled with his carry-on and mumbled something I couldn't make out. He saw the same movie! What feelings did it evoke for him? Did he wonder if it was prophetic? I remember his eyes; they shone with a strange light when he turned away.

Monday, December 7

I listen to the tape of the service Pastor Dan provided for the children here. I reach for understanding of what it was like for them so far removed from the death scene. I hear Dan say, "We wouldn't want him back." Not want their father back? They wouldn't want their youthful, fun-loving father back into their lives? Wouldn't want a grandpa present for their little ones? They'll spend a lifetime nursing an empty spot where their father/grandfather would be. Oh, to have him back for one hour! One hour to talk, ask his advice, ask about his last weeks, days, his last few minutes.

Dan spoke on Romans 8:28, *our* verse—God works for good in all things. It's difficult right now for me to think that anything good can come from Peter's death. But I can truly say the marriage was for good. The relationship made us what we became. It may have been that much better had we been better servants, but marred vessels are the order of the day. God works in spite of our foibles. Vanauken says in *A Severe Mercy* that pain and love go together—you can't have one without the other and the love is worth the pain.

I look through the slides again that Peter took in Australia. It's a set of sunrises and sunsets and gravestones.

Saturday, December 12

I seem to be emerging from the fog. The reality of his absence slices like knives through my being. I'm in a dark, pain-filled place. I feel fragile, frightened. To survive seems impossible, the future too heavy to carry. It's been six weeks and he's starting to fade. Up to now it seemed he was here or would appear at any moment. I could almost sense his body in the house. Now there's a distancing. I can't hear his chuckle any more. I panic to think I may forget what he looked like, what his voice sounded like. I look at his picture and it's as if I'm looking at a relative who was here for a visit. *Yes, he was here; it was so good; remember how we did this and that?*

Joanne drops in. She says to think in terms of twenty or thirty years without him is too crushing. I need to remember, "One day at a time, sweet Jesus, that's all I'm asking of You."

Judy calls to invite me to accompany them to hear Handel's *Messiah*. Christmas! I feel nauseous to think of it but force myself to carry up some boxes of decorations. I find the favourite cone wreath, hang it above the mantel, but then it's all too much. I collapse in the blue rocker to scribble down my feelings:

The flowers have wilted, the thank you notes have all been mailed. Emptiness reigns. The sympathy cards stand tired and disorganized on the mantel, crowding your picture and a bare cone wreath.

In two weeks it's Christmas and I need to decorate. But I don't hear you stomping the snow off your boots while you drag in yet another crooked Christmas tree, insisting with your gay abandon that all its imperfection can be camouflaged with tinsel. You're not here to admire the decorated hearth, to light the fire and the candles, to sit and hold my hand as in quiet wonder we contemplate the warmth of Christmas.

Sunday, December 13

I read an editorial in a church paper on Isaiah 11:1: "A shoot will come up from the stump of Jesse; from his roots a Branch will bear fruit."

Frankl said, "To live is to suffer. To survive is to find meaning in the suffering." The quote, the prophet's words, combined with Joanne's visit yesterday, prompt this:

I am stumped.
The depth of grief and tears not known till now
has leeched all life and hope—
my harp is out of reach.
Adrift, I sit and remember the "timberrrr"
and almost despair that life must go on.
Grace, unspeakable grace, plants a tiny seed,
waters it with the tear-filled eyes of a friend—
Forth shoots a quivering ray of hope
that from this very stump
some fragrant fruit may grow.

Monday, December 14

At 8 o'clock the telephone rings—can't quite catch the caller's name. "A package has arrived in the mail. We're awaiting your instructions."

I struggle to find meaning—it's Christmas; packages arrive. Suddenly the nonsensical words line up to tell their message and I gasp—Peter in a package!

I replace the phone in its cradle and plunk my head on the kitchen counter.

No! No! No!

Strangely, I sense Peter's chuckle. Not in a log after all, but in a package!

His sense of humour bordered on the macabre sometimes.

Years ago, Peter burst into our farmhouse kitchen next door with "I found it!"

"Found what?"

"My coffin."

"Please! Stop it!"

"Look!" He pointed out the window to a tree trunk he'd rolled to the yard's edge. "It's just the right size, and it's already hollow."

"This is *not* nice!" I said, turning away.

He laughed and went back out. He placed half barrels on each side of the log, planted geraniums and ivy in them, and told many of his "find." He saw humour where others see harsh reality. Or he needed to see humour to cope with harsh reality.

I've been looking at his "coffin" now for at least eight years. The new owners of the farm left the log where Peter rolled it; it makes a nice division between yard and woods. I can even see it from this house in winter when the shrubs along the creek are bare.

We'll bury his ashes on Wednesday—in the cemetery.

"Give me relief from my distress; be merciful to me and hear my prayer" (Psalm 4:1).

Wednesday, December 16

And now, the fourth worst day—a burial seven weeks later. It feels as if it all happened yesterday. It's a cold wintry day—an icy wind blows in my soul.

We stand in a small circle, chilled and stilled. My brother-in-law reads Scripture and offers a prayer. The small box Jim and I picked out is placed into the ground. I shudder—reduced to ashes and a piece of paper bearing his name. My future without him looms before me like a yawning hole a thousand times larger than this small space dug in the ground. I remember the prayer Pastor Jack prayed for us at the memorial service: "That they may process the loss of his presence." Process—whatever that means. *Grief work.*

We spend the rest of the day together as a family, find comfort in each other's presence, in the warmth of the fire. It's good we finally experience some closure.

~ Peter's prayer in the *Prayer Diary*:
for all our kids
for Angie
for help…
for blessing…

Thanks, Hon. It was a rough day. Just to read that you prayed for us somehow transcends the time it was written. And yes, there was help; and yes, there was blessing.

Saturday, December 19

Pardon the language, Lord, but I've had a hell of a day. Someone tried to put me on a guilt trip when from this very source I was looking for under-standing and acceptance. Don't they know how much I hurt? And it's Christmas this week, Lord, and I just buried him last week. It's all too much. I feel run over; I can't breathe; I can't see any light. The cold wind bites my face. Where is he, Lord, him whom I have loved? Where is com-

fort? How do I experience the comfort You promise? I can't feel it—there are no arms around me—there's no shoulder to cry on...

The telephone rings—a friend extending sympathies...

The phone rings again—a loving sister to check if I'm OK, reassuring me of understanding and support.

The phone rings a third time—an invitation to a fancy restaurant with dear friends tomorrow.

The phone rings once more...

OK, Lord, I get the message—your comfort is extended to me through human hands and voices. Four calls within two hours of my lowest hour! Did You prompt them all to call tonight? Or was this again a case of "Before you ask, I will answer?"

Hell fades. Heaven breaks through.

Thursday, December 24

In church tonight we sang "Come to my heart, Lord Jesus, there's room in my heart for Thee."

Lord, may this gaping space not be filled with undue grief or self-pity, but may there truly be room for You this empty Christmas.

Friday, December 25

I prepare the turkey early this morning and place it in the oven. The children come and cook the rest of our Christmas dinner.

We gather around the table. I sit in Peter's chair.

"It's one step at a time," I say. "I can't pray today."

David assumes the responsibility and prays, acknowledging Peter's absence and our loneliness.

We tidy up, play games. We make an effort, but we're all so painfully aware of the emptiness we can't fill. I feel bowled over by the extent of our loss. The kingpin of the family has been knocked out and we struggle with the immensity of the hollow space. He was a tower of strength and joy. How will we all survive?

~Prayer Diary:

Peter's note was written a year ago. Our names all over the page! It's as if he's telling me we're all in his heart today. His prayer: *Thank you, Lord, for such a family. We continue to pray that each of us would honour You as our God and Lord.*

We'll try, Hon. We'll try.

Sunday, December 27

Two months today. I wake at 5 o'clock, distraught–had a lovely dream that everything had been a mistake and Peter was alive.

The fact of his being gone is still so hard to accept. I reel against it; I cry for him to be here, to talk just once more, to be held again. I didn't realize how important he was to me, how much fun it was, how good it was to have him with me all the time.

I decide to look up what *comfort* means. The word means to come alongside. A comforter is one who comes alongside and walks with you. Peter was alongside, physically, emotionally, spiritually. With him gone, I'm wobbly and shaky and need others to come alongside and walk with me for a few moments. I think of the dear ones who have done just that, who have offered genuine comfort simply by being present.

I sit alone
to ponder my aloneness
on my mourning bench.
It's carved of stone–cold and hard
placed out of reach of everything
warm and soft and lovely
(or so it seems).
Some pass by and look the other way.
Some stop and tell me how to sit,
how to get up and even leave
this place of tears.

They do not understand its purpose
nor know I have no need
of words, advice or platitudes.
You come and quietly just sit with me
and for a moment feel the contours
of this bench and share my pain.
And I am helped.

Monday, December 28

I've cried nonstop the last two weeks. A river of tears. My eyes are a mess. I catch a glimpse of myself as I walk past the hall mirror and pull back in dismay. I look pale and gaunt and ten years older. Grief is demanding. Tiredness has lodged deeper than bone. The Psalmist agrees: "I am worn out from groaning; all night long I flood my bed with weeping and drench my couch with tears. My eyes grow weak with sorrow…the LORD has heard my weeping" (Psalm 6:6-8).

~Prayer Diary:

Catherine Marshall's prayer: "Therefore, very simply, Lord, I ask You for the gift of faith–the capacity, the ability and the stamina–to trust You for anything the New Year holds. Thank You that this greatest gift of faith is Yours to bestow."

Tuesday, December 29

My lace-curtained bedroom is very bright this morning. I slowly turn around and gaze on a pure white blanket of fresh-fallen snow. The usual gleeful shout of delight is nothing more than a sad wistful sigh. Another first. Snow without Peter won't be the same. The cold harsh landscape not warmed by his presence is just that–cold and harsh. I fear the snow; fear having to shovel myself out; fear getting stuck.

I knock over one of Peter's dried-up plants in the basement. Everything that was his will eventually die.

I've decided not to go back to work until March. I'm giving myself the "luxury" of more time to grieve. The promise is: "Blessed are those who mourn, for they will be comforted" (Matthew 5:4). Also signed up to take two night courses–to keep me occupied and help me to go on living.

Wednesday, December 30

This is a better day again. There hasn't been a day without mail or someone calling or stopping in. The letters I've received are precious. How good of people to share their memories of Peter, things I didn't even know about him! Much of what they write pertains to his generosity, some small deed done long ago: tucking pennies in all four pockets of a little girl's new pair of jeans, dropping a quarter in a little boy's new wallet: *After our [Sunday school] class had a Christmas get-together, Peter asked me what I had received in the gift exchange. I showed him my new wallet. Peter stopped the car, took a quarter out of his wallet and put it in mine. And although it was probably not the first quarter I owned, it is the first one I remember owning. I was a rich little boy. I walked to the house on air that night. Every other detail melts into the mist of that night, but that supposedly twenty-five-cent gesture remains a huge, and one of my fondest, recollections.*

Walking around the block, I notice the beautiful sunset and burst into tears. *Hon, look at the sunset; do you see it?* I guess sunsets and sunrises will always be linked to Peter. For that matter, moons also– actually, is there anything that's not linked to him? Connections, connections, a thousand connections, now all severed. An axe fell and brutally cut all the threads. Each bleeding end needs to be attended to in order to heal.

"You, O God, do see trouble and grief; you consider it to take it in hand" (Psalm 10:14).

Thursday, December 31

The last day of this year. I've lived years since Oct. 27th. I'm invited to a New Year's Eve party and am anxious to have "normal eyes." An acquaintance, recently widowed, bravely invited all his friends because this is something his wife did every year. His courage encourages me. There is life after death. Friends shower me with hugs. It feels overwhelming to be in the midst of a large group of people—the noise, the music. My mind reels with all the conversation.

Someone says, "You don't look like a widow." *What am I supposed to look like?*

The midnight hour approaches. The lump in my throat thickens. I'm nervous—visualize the midnight moment. How will I manage without "losing" it? Another widow seeks me out. "Let's sit here," she says, "let's not look." She leads me to a loveseat facing a window. We busy ourselves with exaggerated chit-chat, our backs turned to all the kissing couples when the hour strikes.

"You gave me life and showed me kindness, and in your providence watched over my spirit" (Job 10:12).

3

January

~Prayer Diary:

"Prepare ye the way of the LORD, make straight in the desert a highway for our God" (Isaiah 40:3, KJV).

Catherine Marshall prays that the Lord may find a clean, warm, responsive abode in her, and help her face the New Year with courage, enthusiasm, and faith.

I join her in the prayer.

A year of grief stretches before me—a year of "processing the loss of his presence." I dread it, yet I know I have to mourn in order to heal. I must embrace grief and not run from it. The only way to get through is to go through.

We both read Sheldon Vanauken's *A Severe Mercy* some eight years ago. It was the first time I faced the hot, searing pain grief brings. I was home alone and cried all day reading the book. Sheldon grieved the death of his wife, Davy, full throttle: faced the grief head-on, faced the whole meaning of the loss, drank the cup, plumbed the depths. I'll pick up his book again—when I feel up to it.

I read Kübler-Ross decades ago after my dad died. Her theory describes stages of grief: shock, denial, bargaining, anger, depression, acceptance. I can relate to the first two: the shock, the denial–it can't be true. Am I bargaining now? If I do the grief work expertly like a good student, then God will restore life to me? A good bargain!

Many take issue with the stages theory and say it's more accurate to think of grief as a series of tasks to be completed: accept the death, feel the emotions, learn to live without the loved one. There is not a neatly laid-out plan to follow.

It's one thing to read and understand the process; it's quite another to experience it!

I've been picturing grief as a desert journey. Peter died in the desert and now I have to walk all the way out of a desert. But I'm challenged to have room for the King.

> *Lord, this desert is so vast, the emptiness so deep,*
> *the barrenness so painful.*
> *It's dry and hot and there's nothing here to quench my thirst.*
> *I'm stranded and feel too weak to traverse this terrain.*
> *They tell me it will be a year before I reach some grass and shady trees.*
> *But someone shouts: "In this desert prepare the way for the Lord!*
> *Make room in this wilderness a highway for your God."*
> *And so, Father, help me to make room in this desert of grief*
> *for Your presence. I need not wander lost and aimless*
> *but can depend on You to lead me on and out.*

Monday, January 4

While looking up more Scripture pertaining to the desert, I find my story in Deuteronomy 32:10,11. "In a desert land he found him, in a barren and howling waste. He shielded him and cared for him; he guarded him as the apple of his eye, like an eagle that stirs up its nest and hovers over its young, that spreads its wings to catch them and carries them on its pinions."

> *An unending land of rust-red sand, barren rock, dry riverbeds,*
> *trees and shrubs struggling to survive, sun scorching man and beast.*

In the centre of this lifeless desert, death pounces and relentlessly
robs me of the only life I knew, leaving me deserted,
empty, barren, trembling, afraid. But a stranger draws near–
kindly speaks and gently leads. Others come
and stand alongside to comfort, care and guide.
A gentle voice penetrates my pain:
In a desert land He found her, in a barren and howling waste
He shielded her and cared for her;
He spread his wings and carried her.

Wednesday, January 6

What a down day! The bitter cold echoes the misery inside. All this mess to clean up. Don't have the energy or ambition to clean up my dishes–how can I ever tackle closets full of Peter's things? Finally found Smedes' book *How Can It Be All Right When Everything Is All Wrong?*

I wanted to read his chapter on joy with pain. He says joy is a feeling that it's all right with us even when everything seems wrong. I list all the things that have given me joy despite the pain. Seventeen in all! Everything from the man who came to the campground to the gift of a job waiting when I arrived home.

There's a shift in reality when we count our blessings. But we can close ourselves to joy.

Monday, January 11

At Ruth Anne's with Wayne for soup and games. We decide to make it a regular Monday event–forming new patterns, new rituals.

Last weekend I kept thinking of Peter as my coach, pushing me to prepare for widowhood. He often talked about it, even though the talk was, true to character, cloaked in joking and teasing. (There's a nice toothless old man for you!)

He called me to come outside one day last spring with one of his "I have something I want to show you" lines. I followed him to the driveway. He had the car hoisted up. "I want to show you how to check and change the oil." I turned on my heels and marched back up the steps and said, "I do *not* need to know that!" He called back, "How are you ever going to survive if you don't know how to check the oil?"

He was concerned, encouraged, comforted and the last six weeks were like a respite to store up energy. He tucked a love note in my pocket, told me his last joke, and left so peacefully. Even though he's absent now, I sense him coaching me still with the presence of his influence. He'll be there at the Finish, welcoming, smiling, whispering, "I knew you could do it!"

Tuesday, January 12

One of the night courses begins. After a lengthy introduction, the professor asks us to draw three balloons and in them picture our work, our play, and our dreams. Work and play are no problem. But my dreams? I try to draw a map of Australia. Cape York juts out too far.

We have to share. I mutter something about dreaming to go back to Australia. Everyone must know what my true dream is. I flee the class at break.

Another professor "corners" me and asks about my "loss." He says my eyes are clear and therefore I must have grieved properly. Am I an object of their studies? And he said "grieved," past tense. I've only just begun!

"You hear, O LORD, the desire of the afflicted; you encourage them, and you listen to their cry" (Psalm 10:17).

Wednesday, January 13

The fog I've been in is starting to evaporate; the valley walls that have obstructed my view are starting to collapse. I have a clearer view of the landscape and the loss of married life looms like a mountain too immense to ever scale.

Someone at church said to think of my relationship with Peter as something very precious that is stored in a special place. He motioned with his hands as if to place a box on a shelf.

I hold that picture and it comforts me. Our relationship, the privacy of it, the beauty of it, preserved as a treasure in a gold-covered box. I'll carry a precious personal treasure with me the rest of my life. The picture comforts but it also brings me closer to the core of my grief–the contents of the beautiful box.

The Little Prince said, "It is such a secret place, the land of tears" (de Sainte-Exupéry).

Friday, January 15

Wayne comes and offers to go through Peter's clothes. I need to help; it's part of the grief work.

> *I find a big box to put your suits in.*
> *No big deal, it just must be done.*
> *So I fold the first jacket and lower it in*
> *and suddenly it's you I'm lowering again–*
> *again and again and again.*
> *The pain of our parting is upon me once more;*
> *the tearing, the searing, the aching so sore.*
> *I clutch a favourite and sit down to sob*
> *resting my head as so often I've done*
> *against the tweed jacket–*
> *but something is wrong.*
> *It's empty–you're gone.*

"Keep me safe, O God, for in you I take refuge" (Psalm 16:1).

Monday, January 18

~*Prayer Diary*:

Peter's prayer: *Father, in the quietness of this hour and in the secrecy of my closet, I come to ask You to continue to demonstrate Your power in* our midst. *In time of physical death, will You bring new life into hearts and lives of individuals and homes? Father, You heard the heart's cry to You for Your grace.*

He prayed this in response to the death of a young girl. His words encourage me today.

Tuesday, January 26

Hon, it'll be three months tomorrow. I remember your sigh and the terrible fact that one minute you were joking and the next minute you were gone. The hairdresser's hand brushed my cheek today. I trembled with shock to feel the warmth and blinked away tears as I realized the depth of my longing for you.

Everyone seems to be monitoring me. Am I crying too much? Not enough? "You must let go." "I hope you're not on medication." "You must take something." "Are you sitting around and moping?" "You must get out more." "You must take time to be alone." I'm so tired of all the advice. They don't know. I so desperately wish you were here to keep my thinking straight. How do I carry on? I search every page of your diary for some message you left behind. I'm sure you had no idea I'd devour it now. It's such a gift to know what you were thinking and praying; to see your quest to live close to God. I see things I didn't understand before. You cared so much.

I wept three months ago beside that hospital bed. My tears tonight come from a much deeper place. Will it get worse? Or, is this the bottom? Will it ever improve?

Wednesday, January 27

I'm so tired, Lord. It's been three months. At first I thought I could make it, studied the terrain, made sure I had the right equipment. Now I'm not sure of anything and wonder if I'll get through. Why do I have to go this way? Why did I have to leave the grassy slopes and shelter and sunshine to tread this weary path while others enjoy life and love?

"Give ear to my words, O LORD, consider my sighing." "How long must I wrestle with my thoughts and every day have sorrow in my heart?" (Psalm 5:1; 13:2).

A walk with Josh:

Look, Grandma, there's a bird.
He let go of my hand, brushed away the snow
to uncover a small sparrow lying
at the side of the road.
It's dead, Grandma.
He picked it up and held it tenderly
in mittened hands, stroking its feathers.
The wings don't flap any more, Grandma.
It's all dead.
Maybe a car hit it. Let's bring it home.
We walked on, the now serious three year old
carefully carrying the tiny stiff body.
We climbed the steps to the door.
Let's bring it inside, Grandma,
and we can warm it up.
No, Josh, we need to leave it out here,
we need to put it in the ground.
Oh, no, Grandma!
Well, let's leave it on the porch
so we can see it a little while longer
and tomorrow we'll put it in the ground.
OK. The wings don't flap any more.
It's dead, isn't it?
Yes, dear, it's dead.

4

February

I seem to be at a different level. I've moved from an all-positive attitude toward Peter to a more realistic one. There were negatives. I wonder how much of this I need to work through, the total package. Sheldon Vanauken reread all their journals during his "grief work." I can do the same: put the relationship in perspective; see the meaning of it; come to terms with its stains and flaws; acknowledge the tensions and struggles of two separate people making life together, being married. Healing means to let go, forgive, accept things as they were, lay it to rest.

Leafing through the prayer diary, I look for my name. He wrote so much that I knew nothing of. April's pages contain many entries about me: all *thanks* and *please bless her* and *make her a blessing; she's a virtuous woman,* etc., etc.

The entry that grabs me he wrote while I did a three-week teaching stint for my degree. It was a difficult three weeks, but Peter laughed and chided how easy and simple it all was. Now I read his prayers for me: *Help Angelina in her three-week teaching block. Help me to give her all the support she needs.* Later: *Bless her, continue to make her a blessing.* And a few days after that: *Thank You, Lord, for the way you help Angie with her teaching.*

He wrote all this, thought all this, prayed all this, yet toward me he acted almost disinterested with his breezy, "There's nothing to it!"

His heart, his heart of love, hidden behind a joking, chiding facade. I'm privileged now to have this window to his soul, yet how much easier it would've been had I been able to see this, hear this, then.

Tonight in class, our instructor elaborates on the difficulties one faces in a marriage. I sense he's sharing the challenges he's facing in his remarriage to a much younger mate. He keeps glancing my way. Is he sending a message? Be thankful your struggles are over? *(I'll gladly take any struggles to have Peter back!)* Or, be careful, don't rush into another relationship? Or is he giving me permission to admit all was not sunshine and roses?

Monday, February 8

I'm taking a ten-day vacation in L.A. with Ruth Anne, Josh and Kaleb at Kirk's family home. At a wedding on Saturday, someone "complimented" me on being the youngest widow he'd ever seen! Good grief.

I drive to La Jolla today to spend a few days alone. I've brought some favourite authors; I think I'm ready now to reread what they have to say about the grieving process. I'd like to get some grief out of the way so I can go back to work. Maybe it doesn't work that way.

I exult in the beauty of today—the beauty of La Jolla—a picturesque town clinging tenaciously to a hillside above a heaving ocean. The houses on the perpendicular streets look like rock climbers, strung together in long rows.

The cove is a magnificent spot, a sheltered curve of rock, protected from waves that crash white behind the wall of rock. A crescent patch of sand fills the curve of the cove, and it all looks like a giant high-backed armchair where one can nestle, protected from wind and sun.

I've come to an oasis in the desert, a respite, a change of scenery, a place to rest and refresh my tired spirit far away from the cold winter back home. Peter and I stopped here for a cup of coffee two years ago on our way to San Diego. We thought the spot so pretty and decided to come back some time. *Well, I'm here, Hon!*

I climb the hill and find the shops and restaurants. Two books on grief find me.

After watching a blazing sun slide into the water, I snuggle into bed with a cup of tea and read one of the new books, *How to Survive the Loss of a Love* (Bloomfield, Colgrove, McWilliams).

Tuesday, February 9

I take my beach towel and relax in the curve of the rock chair with its soft sand cushion. I've brought the books. There's no way I can read them all today, but I feel a measure of comfort to be surrounded by the authors, knowing friends to accompany me during these "alone" days.

A graph depicts the grief journey—a zigzag line drawn across a page. There's no rhyme or reason to the journey, no neatly laid-out path to follow; rather, it's yo-yo, up and down, highs and lows, good and bad days, tears and sudden laughter.

Judy Tatelbaum in *Courage to Grieve*, the other book I purchased last night, says circumstances affect how we grieve. Courage, knowledge, and support are key factors. It takes huge amounts of courage to face all the emotions that erupt, to give expression to them, to be with the pain.

> *Grief is not an illness,*
> *not a weakness,*
> *not a state of being,*
> *but a process.*
> *Trust the process,*
> *it moves forward.*
> *The only cure for grief is to grieve.*
> *It's a necessity, the flip side of love.*

The book encourages me; I'm on the right track. I relate to the change that comes after the first acute grief. I'm much quieter now. It still comes in waves, but they're further apart and not so overwhelming. Maybe I've travelled a very rough part of the journey. There'll be more. The graph goes up and down.

Evening

I walk along the water to watch another sunset, and find a sheltered spot among the rocks to give way to tears of sadness. I picture grief as a bucket of water that needs emptying. *There, another dipperful is gone.*

Wednesday, February 10

Had a very vivid dream in which Peter was dead. In all my previous dreams, he appeared alive or sick, but not dead. This dream was death, period. There was no questioning, no disbelief. Maybe the dream tells me I've accepted the death as "a fact" at a deep level—the first "task" to be completed.

Lewis *(A Grief Observed)* and many others found God out of reach during the dark days following the death. He felt as if God had bolted a door shut. He realized later that God doesn't shut the door—we do. I felt shut out before Peter's death—I put up the barricades—but that day in Alice a door was swung wide open and my faith was restored. I remember thinking at the end of that day, "I'll never doubt God's presence again."

Thursday, February 11

I'm reading Sheldon Vanauken's *A Severe Mercy* with a new perspective and new tears. I'm again deeply touched by the way he cared for his wife, Davy, how he carried her, carried her fear.

How was it for you, Peter?

*Did I suffer **with** you? Did I enter with you into your pain, feel your anxiety, your frustration, your anger at losses suffered too early in life? Did*

*I walk with you hand in hand on your spiritual journey as you came to grips
with the awesome thought of meeting your Maker?*

*We suffered, your pain and mine—I wish I had let go of mine to enter
more fully into yours.*

Sheldon found God to be very gentle in Davy's dying. How gently He also took care of me in that howling, barren waste! Sheldon
and Davy had the privilege to be able to say goodbye. Heart attack
victims and their families seldom do. One minute here, laughing,
the next minute—gone. My grieving is saying goodbye.

The bereaved search for meaning. Sheldon believed Davy's
death was for his own highest spiritual good because she came
first with him rather than God. The reasoning is so gripping, so
cutting. Our verse: "In all things God works for the good of those
who love him...."

I need a break and dive into the pool, let the water hold me. I
try to cheer myself by singing "One day at a time." I croak the
words, "Yesterday's gone...tomorrow may never be mine." They
don't cheer; they slice. My life—divided into before and after. And
"tomorrow" may never be mine.

Be with the pain, they say; feel its throb, its sting. It will pass.

Friday, February 12

My last day here in La Jolla. On my morning walk I take photos of
the rising sun shining through twisted, gnarled tree branches. It's a
glorious display of shadow and light. The broken, the warped,
bathed in healing Light—a picture of my days here. It feels as though
my heart was sliced open; truth entered; cleansing happened—a step
toward healing.

I long to share with Peter what I've read, what I've learned, the
many pages I've written. Maybe he knows. Sheldon felt that Davy
did know and even longed for him. He sensed her presence with
him for two years after her death. The essence was that she was present to be of help to him. He had a very vivid detailed dream in
which she affirmed this. C.S. Lewis wrote to him and shared that he

also felt his deceased wife's strong presence from time to time; she could do more for him now than before. He felt that maybe God gave the deceased a gift on arrival in heaven—some great blessing to the beloved they'd left behind.

I think of my own dream in which Peter had all the answers, brought me tea. Is he allowed to be near? Is he reading over my shoulder? Is it because of him that these days have been so beneficial? How I long for the curtain to be drawn aside for a moment. But: "No eye has seen, no ear has heard..." (1 Corinthians 2:9).

I watch the sunset and then drive back to L.A. I need to talk again, play with the boys—give and receive hugs and kisses.

"But the LORD was my support. He brought me out into a spacious place... (Psalm 18:18,19).

Sunday, February 14

I rise before anyone else is up. This "first" is unexpected. Didn't think Valentine's Day to be important, yet there is grief welling up and I'd best get out on the lonely streets to shed the pent-up tears. It's a beautiful Sunday morning; a pink sun is rising, there's a warm breeze, and gardens are blooming with spring flowers.

I find a café, buy a cup of coffee, and sip it sitting on a garden wall.

Peter was a romantic—loved to surprise me with gifts, usually roses. Thirteen at a time; we were married on a Friday the 13th. Ruth Anne received a rose from Kirk yesterday and that triggered it all. No roses for me this year.

I must have a rose; he would want me to have a rose today. I wander around, find a flower shop, but only have $1.50 in my pocket after I bought the coffee.

"The roses are $2.00," the dark-haired saleslady informs.

"I only have $1.50. Would you make an exception?"

"Sorry, they're $2.00."

"I really need a rose."

"I could let you have an open one for $1.00."

"That would be great, thank you."

She wraps it in cellophane with some greenery and I leave, inhaling its delicate fragrance.

"Where did you get the rose?" Kirk's mother asks me when I gently lay it on the kitchen table.

"A rose dropped down from heaven," I say
as I gaze at the rich red circles of petals glistening
with mist in the morning sun. The aroma moistens
my cheek as I remember thirty years of roses arriving
in lavish bunches of thirteen or six or three or only one—
a token of his love to grace our home. Yet this lone red beauty
in this desert land somehow smells sweeter than the rest,
as it speaks to me of love perfected,
now that he's gained the eternal quest.

This afternoon we go for a drive and as I glance out the car window, I see a small aircraft circling to complete a large white feathery heart on an intense blue sky. I have the uncanny feeling that Peter ordered this tiny plane to draw this great big heart for me to see—a message of love in the heavens for me.

Tuesday, February 16

After a long day travelling, I arrive home at midnight. I crawl into his chair and reach for the prayer diary. I felt so anxious about the future on the way home—holidays are over, back to work; I'm on my own. I find today's page and read: "Therefore do not worry about tomorrow, for tomorrow will worry about itself. Each day has enough trouble of its own" (Matthew 6:34).

Peter's note was written in '81. *Lord you know I've been anxious. Forgive, because I know you have everything planned for our good!*

How often it occurs: what I read is just what I need!

Thursday, February 18

Almost bewildered that I feel strong, rested and confident at the new job. It's exhilarating to focus on work to be done, courses to design, people to serve.

~*Prayer Diary*:
"Now go; I will help you speak and will teach you what to say" (Exodus 4:12).

Peter's prayer: *Be with our mouths and help us to speak words of encouragement and words that help.*

Thanks, Hon, for this confirmation.

Sunday, February 21

This day was long and tiring, filled with good things, yet at the end of it I'm grasping for more. Something is missing. I can't share with Peter—can't tell him all about it—and that leaves a strange emptiness and meaninglessness to it all. "I have become like a bird alone on a roof" (Psalm 102:7).

I've lost my love, my soulmate, my best friend, the one with whom to share meals, books, tiny incidents of a day. I've lost the one who looked after the finances, who mowed the lawn, took the garbage out and kept the car serviced. I've lost the one who carried the joyful spirit in this house, the one who led us spiritually.

Someone said, "The love that is now lost is the love that will sustain you and lead you to life and healing."

~*Prayer Diary*:
Peter's comment on the mustard seed parable: *Before you give up: help that tiny seed of faith to grow into a plant where others will not only rest but also find shelter and security.*

Monday, February 22

I met a fellow traveller today and we shared the difficulties of our journeys, but it was obvious his way was easier than mine, or so it seemed. The few tufts of grass in his part of this desert appeared greener than mine. I was envious—until I looked again and noticed travellers who had no grass at all.

Tuesday, February 23

First appointment with a grief counsellor—decided to give myself this "gift."

I leave the session feeling calmer, stronger, affirmed. I've been trying so hard to get it just right, to get an "A" on this grief course. This has its advantages but can also be a snare. The achiever in me may be hindering the healer. Give the healer a voice. Listen to her; she will gentle you forward. Can't hurry the process. Give it the time it needs.

I need to block time each day for grief. Time to remember, read, cry, pray, write, whatever. Then leave it, knowing I'll get back to it the next day. This will free me up to live, to work, even to enjoy whatever the day may bring.

The counsellor says to expect more low points: six months, one year. I hope this doesn't become a self-fulfilling prophecy.

He asks, "Are you 'alone' or 'all one'?"

I have to be alone
to become all one.
Whole.
Someone special torn from me
leaves me feeling like one half of
whole.
To remain one half
means searching for another half
to make a whole.
To be all one and

meet another one
will be a dance
a song of whole fulfillment.
Healing will fill full the hole.
Therefore
I'm going to heal!

Thursday, February 25

The ladies thank me after my talk tonight and ask, "You lost your husband four months ago? How can you speak and laugh? Are you medicated?"

No. Two people inhabit my body. One is a "strong lady," talking, laughing. On the drive home her tears begin to flow. The front door yawns open. The walls cry his absence. Silence hugs the furniture like a shroud. A snivelling two-year-old steps into the house and cries out for someone to hold her. A little girl sobs herself to sleep, clutching his pillow like a teddy bear. She doesn't know who spoke so confidently tonight. That person must dwell within somewhere.

Tomorrow as I approach the office I'll coax her to reappear. Sighing helps. I'm sighing so much lately. (Body craving oxygen? Grief seeking to be breathed out?) One deep breath helps to bring her back. I'll open the door and greet everyone cheerfully. With some effort, the "strong lady" stays in place for the day, but too many questions bring the snivelling two-year-old out of hiding.

When will I be "whole" again?

Correction: I *am* whole. Grief is part of who I am right now.

"My sighing is not hidden from you" (Psalm 38:9).

Sunday, February 27

Yesterday I thought the 27th wouldn't bother me this month, but a tide of grief wells up again today. Dave comes to stay the night and shows me the slides he took of the family here after Peter's death. Sadness grips me as I think of their grief. One beautiful slide of them strolling through the leaves reminds me again that it was fall when he fell.

169

*It was fall
when you fell.
Now it is winter.
Then spring
without your return
and summer
without your warmth.
When the leaves are falling
I will remember
it was fall when you fell
—and rose.*

5

March

~*Prayer Diary*:

Peter scribbled Isaiah 43:18,19: "Forget the former things; do not dwell on the past. See, I am doing a new thing! Now it springs up; do you not perceive it? I am making a way in the desert and streams in the wasteland."

People are leaving; reality has come home to roost. The crying has been so intense but–look–a roadway and a river in my desert, leading to something new!

Peter added: *I want to be in the centre of that adventure when you do the new thing!*

First there were many who walked with me to help me on my way. Most have gone, busy with their own affairs, except for a faithful few and I'm so careful not to impose lest they also tire.

Does this mean from here on I travel alone? It reminds me how we used to accompany a friend halfway home after school. But, I'm not halfway yet.

Sunday, March 6

I saw a gracious Lord finding, carrying, a wounded soul.
I saw a sweet surrender to the Master's will,
a noble thought that fruit would grow from pain.
I saw courage to tread this desert path, following His lead.
A cloud has come; the view is gone.
All this darkness reveals is a harsh, demanding God
requiring the ultimate sacrifice and an angry
rebellious soul, reeling with pain, thrashing about,
blaming others, and screaming, "Why?"

Friday, March 11

I seem to have wandered off the beaten path. I feel lost, helpless—as if I'm a cork bobbing at the mercy of the waves. Things aren't going according to plan. My expectations of others are continually dashed to pieces. They keep asking, "What's the matter?" when I say I'm not feeling all that well. Have they all forgotten?

I grab a piece of paper and draw my own grief graph. A broken line along the top. A crazy zigzag line beneath that slowly goes up. I add all the words that describe the feelings I've experienced and probably will yet experience. I want to say to everyone, "See, you're living along the top line. I'm way down here in the valley. *That's* what's the matter! Give me time. It'll take awhile before I'm back to where you are."

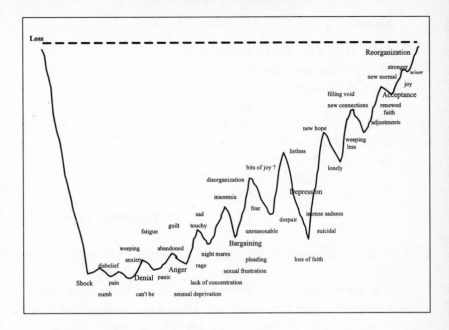

March's Anger

The void
unspeakable
incomprehensible
screams
to be filled.
The scream
inaudible
unbearable
gives birth
to anger.
The anger
unsustainable
irrational
finds
a target.

Alone?

Alone, alone, I cry, I'm all alone!
No one cares or understands.
Anger obstructs; despair is dark
and hides from view the armies of the Lord.
"Count, my child, count the many I have sent
to surround you, to encourage you, to care for you."
I lift downcast eyes and count
and bow in humble gratitude.

Tuesday, March 21

At the dentist paying my bill, I tell the secretary, "My husband has died."

"I'm sorry," she says and reaches for a tiny bottle, pulls out a brush and before my very eyes, with a few deft strokes, erases him; wipes him out with whiteout. It only takes a moment.

I'm glad his name is "engraved in rock forever."

Wednesday, March 30

There's a different climate of feeling with the passing of another month. The tears are drying up. I don't reach out for him as much and that in itself brings sadness. He always seemed to be here; it felt as if he surrounded me. I contemplated him, saw his beauty, the beauty of the person. Now it feels as if he's gone. There is just a cold, empty, dusty house. I seem to be mourning two departures: his real presence and his felt one.

Jean, a new friend, widowed a few years ago, has become my lodestar. Her quiet grace, her smile, encourage me that someday I'll arrive where she is. "I think I'm healed," she simply says. My grief counsellor says I'm launched. Put out to sea–slowly leaving the shore where Peter is.

Grief is circular. I can expect to return to places in this journey where I've already been, but this new feeling of happiness, fleeting though it is, is an indication that the circling of grief now has extended to a place where I begin to experience the joy of healing. There are short stretches of time when he's not in my thoughts. Even the diary hasn't exuded his presence this last week. Did his presence really linger to give me comfort? Sometimes it was as if I relaxed against him when I sank into his chair. I tell my counsellor I feel as if a leaf has been turned.

"Little by little we start to come alive" (Frederick Buechner).

Softly, ever so softly
spring slipped into my soul today.
The sun's warm rays, the morning mist
coaxed cold dark earth so recently buried
in snow and ice to soften
and release the first bright blossom
of spring.
It sat so precarious on slender stem
in the drab grey dirt, but there it was—
a touch of glory heralding a new beginning!

Thursday, March 31

The desert is so still today. Storms and anger have subsided. People have departed but the mourning doves have come. Their low, haunting call fills the yard this morning. Every spring, I feel a strange sense of foreboding when I first hear their sombre-noted song. Today they seem to moan: we know; we've come to empathize, to help you weep.

And so I plod alongside grief in step with their lament.

6

April

Easter Sunday, April 3

How can it rain on Easter Sunday? How can it be that the most joyful is transformed into the most joyless? The one who brought sunshine to my life is gone, and today my grief-stricken heart is not open to any other light.

"My tears have been my food day and night" (Psalm 42:3).

Saturday, April 9—Birthday

I sit here surrounded by flowers, friends, presents, food, laughter and conversation. I don my mask and smile, while all the while my mind is preoccupied with his presents, and all my being cries out for his presence.

Saturday, April 16

The Alice Springs campground "scene" was before my eyes again most of today. It was triggered by a friend telling us her bird had died of a heart attack. Others joked about giving it mouth-to-mouth or inventing tiny paddles to shock the heart. They howled with laughter. I'm glad I can sit through something like that now without having to escape.

Tuesday, April 19

Something is different today. I find an old telephone notebook in which we recorded messages. I leaf through it and burst out in laughter instead of tears. It's so pure and clean–a sense of delight as I remember his writing.

On Sunday, I read through his Marriage Encounter notebook, smiling, eyes misty with thankfulness. Tears of pain transformed to tears of joy. The circle of grief is looping ever further.

I heard someone say we find the true person after he's gone. We see the total picture. Our memory of the person is so much more complete than the daily encounters we had with him. In this sense, we have him with us always.

~*Prayer Diary*:

Thank you for Angelina, followed by a list of things for which he's thankful. How I pleaded with him to talk and share and now he has left me with a whole book full!

Saturday, April 23

The children and I go to see *Return to Snowy River*. I revel in the scenery–dry riverbeds, white gleaming gum trees. How did I manage that day in Alice Springs? Why didn't I scream in desperation? Howl through the campsite like the train did a week earlier exactly at 6 o'clock? (I've often thought of that disturbing incident as an omen.) The screaming came much later. I was anaesthetized at first and, thanks to God, the "angels" supported me.

How can it be to sit on a gum tree having a picnic and two days later everything is over? What would it be like if a person knew? We had so much fun that day and the next–what a gift.

A wistful yearning wells up. I want to go back, retrace our steps in Alice. It will help to find meaning, to gain closure.

I'll have to plan it on a weekend so I can attend a service at the church.

Monday, April 25

I cry for people yet three days of constant company
leaves me with no time to cry.
I'm due to go to work but the dam bursts
sending rivulets of mascara-stained tears down my face.
Oh, well, this morning I'll look a mess at work.
After all, mourning is messy work!

Tuesday, April 26

Jean and I attend THEOS–They Help Each Other Spiritually–a group for the bereaved. A club for the broken-hearted, we say. We expect to meet a group of sad people but noisy talk and laughter greet us–twenty-four ladies, four men. We're divided into groups according to how long we've been bereaved: one year and under, two years, three, four, five and over. *Five years?*

I'm in "newly bereaved." There's a sense of oneness, understanding. We weep in the same language. I've been constantly explaining what I'm going through. These all understand completely! Our experiences are so similar. We're told, "Grief comes in one size only–extra large."

Tonight's topic is how to cope with anger. A punching bag and screaming chamber are good to have. Some say they drive their car to a lonely place and scream. I confess to flinging a mug into the sink and breaking it. The lady next to me whispers, "Only a mug? I broke a whole set of dishes!"

I chat with someone in "five and over." "I put my grief on hold," she says. "Never dealt with it, ran away from it. But I got stuck and now I'm finally being freed up to go on living."

Her words sink in.

One of the nicer-looking men comes to sit beside me. He needs a partner for several upcoming social functions. I politely decline. I don't want to be reduced to a social convenience.

Wednesday, April 27

Six months today. Peter noted in the diary:
Started to dismantle house in Vineland...

At the beginning of April last year, Peter burst into our house with "Look what I found." He waved a tiny piece of paper under my nose, plunked it on the table. It offered someone all the materials and contents of a wooden house just for taking it down. He urged me to come along to look it over. We found the house, alone in a field, dilapidated, its wood siding devoid of paint.

"It's too much work, Hon," I said.

"I can do it. I'll take it slow. I'll use the trailer and bring it all home one load at a time."

"It's too much," I said again.

"No, look at the beautiful staircase, range, claw-foot tub; look at all the kindling and firewood we'll have. We can use the chimney bricks to build a wall in our basement family room. Imagine the beams we'll find!" His excitement was contagious.

"I'll help," I finally said.

And so it was that we spent a fun day there last year on the 27th. No one wanted to be the first to tear off one of the planks. We petted the farmer's horse instead, ate sandwiches and the kids took pictures of Peter and me sitting on the back stoop with long put-on faces. They dubbed us "Pa and Ma Kettle."

Peter was left to tear down the house mostly by himself. Our yard filled with piles of what he called "building materials." He even brought foundation stones home. We took the rest to the lake and rolled the boulders down the bank. As with everything else, it soon became a game.

"Mine rolled farther than yours!" Peter's laughter rang across the water.

I looked at the pile of rocks at the water's edge and wondered if a hundred years ago someone had come to this very spot to gather stones for a foundation. If so, the stones had now returned from where they came.

Friday, April 29

Ups and downs. The emotional roller coaster is disconcerting. It's as if I'm continually jerked this way and then that. I experience something akin to happiness and then I lose my footing and slide back down deep into the valley. I reach a level of acceptance and suddenly find myself back where I've been. It loops around and around. And the tears keep coming.

I wake with a pounding headache—pain prowling around like the pain of grief. There is no escape. It's all around; there's no going back. I'm in the middle of it; there's no place of rest—it's just there, my constant companion. Is this the six-month low?

No matter what I do, how busy I am, how many I talk to, how many times I go out to eat, it doesn't leave me. I'm nauseated with it. I go through the motions, knowing it will still be my companion after the motion ceases. Nothing, nothing, takes it away. Will I ever heal? What is healing anyway—does it simply mean I'll get so used to the ache I'll get numbed to it?

The rain doesn't help. I stand in the gazebo by the lake and see Peter and our four little ones frolicking in the water, playing on the sand, sauntering along the shore, gathering driftwood. I remember the two of us on a blanket here only last summer—books, kisses, laughter. The beginnings, the endings, and all the rest in-between. A life together now ripped apart.

The cold wind brushes my tears, tosses my hair. *Take deep breaths—maybe the cool air will clear the headache.* Nothing helps. My pain companion is glued to me. Inconsolable yearning threads through this day.

David the psalmist asks: "Why are you downcast, O my soul? Why so disturbed within me? Put your hope in God" (Psalm 43:5).

7

May

Wednesday, May 3

It feels as if I'm blind, traversing this dark terrain. Nothing is familiar; everything has changed. I'm confused, perplexed, afraid, groping; then find a message left for me: "I will lead the blind by ways they have not known, along unfamiliar paths I will guide them; I will turn the darkness into light before them and make the rough places smooth" (Isaiah 42:16).

I relax and pray for courage to follow.

Dreams

Journeying through the night we meet.
We laugh and love and laugh again.
You disappear at dawn.
I cry...
Yet smile to know the dream to be
a memory of reality.

Monday, May 9

I value the concern of co-workers. I've tried to be open as to where I am when they ask, "How are you?"

But today they say, "Leave your grief at home. Don't take it to work."

Puzzled, I feel somewhat betrayed. Maybe I've told too much. They tell me my grief evokes uncomfortable feelings.

I don't respond, feel emptied of any words that would make sense.

C.S. Lewis says the bereaved are a "death head." I represent what will happen to one member of each married couple. I'm a reminder of grief past or grief to come. No one likes to be reminded.

Sometimes I think of my grief as a heavy backpack I try to untie every morning and toss on the kitchen floor before I leave the house. And if that doesn't work, hurl it into the back seat of the car before I reach the office. I try to discard it for the day, but it's part of me, part of who I am just now, and I can't slough it off altogether. It's not possible to carry this grief in secret. It fills all of my being and squeezes through my smiles, my voice, its intonations. Just looking at me reminds people; the black **W** is visible through make-up.

~Prayer Diary:

Catherine Marshall's prayer a few days ago: "Help me to keep quiet and really listen to the quiet voice of Jesus' Spirit within."

I'm glad I didn't defend myself today. Just let it be. I'll put more effort into being my happy, talkative self, not let on how much I hurt. I'll answer the question "How are you?" with the conventional "I'm fine, thank you."

Sunday, May 8—Mother's Day

It's a lovely day, but subdued. Dave and I go for a walk. He's been wanting to talk but, "your grief took precedence, and rightly so."

My grief has submerged my mother role, leaving the children orphaned. Bless them, they've been there selflessly listening, visiting, writing, caring. "Hang in; I'm surfacing."

Tuesday, May 10

I'm rereading *To Live Again* by Catherine Marshall. She writes that God made man and woman for each other—any other way is wrong. To be widowed is like having a "gnawing hunger, a haunting wistfulness at the centre of life…it's always there, always…the need to love and to be loved—that ultimate of life." She asks, "Could I, and all those like me who walk the earth in wistfulness, find the way to trust God even for that?"

Friday, May 13

"And by the way, I don't appreciate you hugging my husband." A click at the other end of the phone line. I replace my receiver and plunk my head on the counter. One more indication of the shattering of my life as it was, who I was. The hug was a small gesture from a good friend, automatic on both sides. Many reach out with a hug just now.

We were a couple, related as a couple to many of our friends. Peter with his joking, outgoing friendliness "carried" many of our relationships. Without him, relationships aren't the same. One side of a square or a triangle is missing. The figure teeters; it may collapse. It has to be rebuilt. It will be different. It may not last.

Betty from THEOS phones—God's timing. She understands. She says stored-up energy runs out at six months; exhaustion sets in and we have a difficult time.

Afternoon

I dry my tears and decide to attend a singles' conference after all. A large part of me resists going. It's admitting that, yes, I'm now single. But part of me wants to check it out.

Relief and surprise. Relief: Everyone here knows the meaning of grief and loneliness and long nights. And walking around with that "haunting wistfulness" in your heart.

Surprise: Many beautiful people inhabit the single world. My personal contact with them has been so limited while I travelled the couple circuit.

We sing: "You, You are my wholeness."

Saturday, May 14

Speakers and workshops at the conference are challenging. The energy invested in Peter has to be rewound into myself. Grief is the pain of drawing the energy away from Peter. Talking about it enables you to take back the energy into yourself.

We don't like the experience of grief. Others don't like us to show grief (!), so we ourselves, as well as society, keep us from grieving.

Healing seems a long way off. He's still in my thoughts every day. So much energy is still flowing out to him, the longing for his presence so intense. Someone said to me, "I remember the morning I made it to the kitchen before I thought of her."

Sunday, May 15

If I should sum up the essence of you I'd say:
"A sunny Sunday in May."
Warm sunshine, soft blue sky, trilling bird chorus...
all of nature on tiptoe in joyful expectation
of the wondrous unfolding of spring.
It's such a Sunday today but your absence
is like a knife-gash through the canvas.

Wednesday, May 18

"Therefore...I will lead her into the desert and speak tenderly to her. There I will give her back her vineyards, and will make the Valley of Achor a door of hope. There she will sing as in the days of her youth..." (Hosea 2:14,15). (*Achor* means trouble.)

This morning there is nothing left.
In vain I've searched for sustenance in this dry and barren land,
tried every spring, ran to each miraged oasis,
talked to countless people, read the books...
I gaze in disbelief. There is nothing, nothing as far as my eye
can see that offers relief from the searing pain within,
and the very strength that bore the pain till now has seeped away.
I've reached the lowest point, I muse. This is the heart of it.
Alone and weak I look about and see a Rock, a cleft therein,
a place to hide. Exhausted, I lean, lean hard, and rest.
The stillness offers a voice—the Rock does speak so tenderly:
"I led you here—this vale of tears and trouble will be a door
of hope to you. I will restore. You'll sing once more
as in the days when you were young.
*Trust me, **this** is the heart of it."*

Saturday, May 21

Hon, I conquered a few more "firsts" today. The yard, your pride and joy, stared at me, defiant with weeds and tall wet grass. The lawnmower, that beastly thing, needed to be choked and kicked and baptized with tears before it sputtered to life. Do you hear it, Hon? Do you hear the noise? I'm doing it! I filled your flower boxes with dirt (I guess they also now are mine) and stepped on two rusty nails, one in each foot. (Products of your little house.) I toyed with death—why not? But late at night with two sore feet, I hobbled to Emergency and during my two-hour wait remembered how you were always there for me when I was sick.

This road alone is scary. Yet, yesterday you jotted in your book: "With God all things are possible."

I'm rereading Katie Wiebe's *Alone: A Search for Joy.* She talks about regrets: we didn't spend time together. Others echo her words: if only we'd stopped to smell the roses. Sheldon Vanauken tells a different story. They took time, unhurried time, to be together—to enjoy each other. They enjoyed sunsets, walks, books, talk. They lived fully; they savoured the moment, the beauty of the moment. Our six weeks in Australia came closest to that, a gift of endless hours to spend together—just being together was all that mattered.

I'm glad we had the time, took the time, to smell the roses! I read through the journals of our three-month California trip—also a stretch of unhurried time of being close, enjoying each moment of the day. Maybe I should write about the two years of retirement we had, the good times we shared: him coming along to the college to sit in on my classes; me dropping everything when he said, "Come outside, I want to show you something."

I would title my piece: *We Stopped to Smell the Roses*.

Thursday, May 26

Tomorrow will be seven months. Sleep still ragged. Morning time in Peter's chair with the diary and the psalms have seen me through many a heavy day. As in yesterday—weighed down with the present and the future looming too heavy to carry, yet in the diary I find: "Blessed be the Lord, who bears our burdens and carries us day by day" (Psalm 68:19, AMP).

I pictured myself carried throughout the day and the thought lightened my step. I remembered how God "carried" me that day in Australia.

"When you see only one set of footprints, it was then that I carried you."

8

June

A difficult start to the day. I call Jean and she encourages me. We talk about our proposed self-help grief group. Self-help means we do it ourselves. No one can do it for us.

Ruth Anne and the boys drop by and she invites me along to Ikea in Toronto. I'm thankful that the distressing beginning of the day can be set aside or simply experienced and I'm enabled to go and enjoy the trip. Months ago, I wouldn't have been able to do this.

~Prayer Diary:
"Many waters cannot quench love, neither can the floods drown it" (Song of Songs 8:7, KJV).

Catherine writes, "O Deliverer, when the overwhelming floods of despair threaten to overtake me, transfer me to the realm of supernatural love. Then the unquenchable fire of your love, caught up by faith, will triumph."

Tuesday, June 14

Looking through Peter's photo albums, I feel overwhelmed that everything he owned, everything about his life, is here in my possession. I'm the guardian of his memory. So many photos are sprinkled with unfamiliar faces. All the information is lost with death. The school pictures aren't dated. I tentatively date and label some. It feels so precarious. What will happen to his things when I pass on? It's like the grass withers and you don't know the place of it any more.

Sunday, June 19—Father's Day

I make it to a church service and the praise songs move me, overwhelm me, to think how much God loves and cares. He will order everything.

The first Father's Day. I have a vision of Peter smiling all day as he's looking down on us. Ruth Anne and the boys come along to the cemetery. With tears, we acknowledge our grief but also our blessings. Ruth Anne says she also pictures Peter smiling at her with the Peachy Keen shop and how he'd be there helping her. Josh asks me, "When are you getting a new Daddy?"

> *Visiting the cemetery—your final resting place they say.*
> *I stand upon the grass and stare upon your name.*
> *It's only a spot that holds the last of your remains.*
> *You are not here; you are alive.*
> *All day I sensed you smiling from above as you watched*
> *us here, seen in a different light.*
> *You saw our love, our plans, our happy talk.*
> *You saw our deep emotion as we bowed in prayer.*
> *You saw our tears, new ventures and new friends.*
> *You saw a little boy still missing you—*
> *You saw—and smiled.*

Wednesday, June 22

Fitful night. Bills not paid. Eaves full of junk. Water pump not working properly. Yard a mess, flowers still not planted. Vacuum still broken, papers not filed, things lost, glasses still lost. I feel as if my whole life is a mess. I'm the sole person in charge of everything. I'm so bone-tired. It would all be so much simpler if Peter were here and things ran like they used to run with him in charge.

I must remember, it's while I'm *in* the desert that He will speak tenderly, give back my vineyards, make the valley of trouble a door of hope.

Sunday, June 26

The house rings with laughter today. The cloud of sadness that hangs over us when we're together as a family lifts today. It's as if a candle were lit in this house of mourning. Kaleb accompanies me home after church simply because he wants to. He stands at the kitchen sink on a chair and peels eggs for the salad like a pro. The others come for lunch. Josh and Kaleb attended the circus and now perform acrobatic tumbles for us on the loveseat. Daniel quietly plays on the floor with Grandma's toys. We fetch photo albums to see how much he resembles his father when he was a baby. Ruth Anne announces she's pregnant again! Julie and Jim are also expecting. We talk about Peter and laugh—how much he'd enjoy two more babies! He put away a gold coin after Dylan was born and said, "Whoever can present me with a granddaughter will receive this." Whose will it be?

Monday, June 27

And now it's eight months. It's a matter of getting used to it. I've gotten used to coming home alone, eating my baked potato, watching the news. Even sleeping alone is not such a big deal any more. Your lifestyle and behaviour adjust, and after awhile it feels somewhat like comfortable. The new single friends and outings have helped tremendously. I'm in a good place right now but wonder how long it will last and what is yet ahead in the journey.

"Blessed are those whose strength is in you, who have set their hearts on pilgrimage. As they pass through the Valley of Baca, they make it a place of springs…. They go from strength to strength, till each appears before God in Zion" (Psalm 84:5-7).

I've been tremendously blessed and encouraged by these words this month!

Our strength lies in God. We can't ever travel this valley in our own strength.

We *set* our hearts on pilgrimage, *set* our hearts to grieve. We *decide* to *go* through it, as that's the only way to *get* through it.

Baca means mourning or grief. The Valley of Baca, real or figurative, was a place pilgrims needed to go through on their way to Jerusalem.

While we go through this valley of grief, it's our responsibility to make it a place of springs. We need to provide refreshment for ourselves. Dig wells. Be gentle with yourself. Find support.

We go from strength to strength. It's one step at a time. It's a process; it moves forward.

Until we appear in Zion—the end of the journey. The time we'll experience healing; the time we'll be healed.

9

July

Today, last year:

Peter opened the front door, leaned against its frame and said, "It's finished."

I knew what he meant–finished tearing down the little house–but the words jolted me. They sounded too much like Jesus' words: "It is finished." I glanced at him and he held my eyes. His face and hair were dusty, his rumpled pants and shirt smeared with dirt. He looked exhausted, waited for my commendation.

"I'm glad," I finally said.

"I picked up every last nail. The farmer helped to smooth the soil with his tractor. You can't even see where the house was."

"Really?"

"It's completely gone."

I didn't answer.

"Well, it's done," he said with a tired, satisfied sigh.

I wondered about that project last year as he set to work, methodically, carefully, unlike his usual manner of working. I see it now as his last work–the dismantling of a house plank by plank, brick by brick. I see how it symbolized Peter's life coming to an end, heartbeat by heartbeat.

Soon his "house" would be no longer.
"...and its place remembers it no more" (Psalm 103:16).

~Prayer Diary:
Finished my project. Thanks for protection, health, and strength to fin-
ish the task.

I add a prayer that I, also, may finish well.

Monday, July 11

~Prayer Diary:
Joshua and I went on our first fishing trip.

I remember the big production last year. Peter instigated enough excitement for ten people to go fishing. Josh observed the preparations with amusement. His grandpa's antics absorbed him more than the anticipated trip, I think. His brown eyes sparkled as Peter explained each piece of equipment they'd need: fishing rod, tackle box, lures, worms, lunch, life jackets. I helped lift our aluminum rowboat on top of the car, and they were off.

Their first fishing trip—their only one.

Saturday, July 16

Another wedding. I steel myself to go through this day, bravely smiling. I'm ushered in, slide beside an acquaintance in a pew close to the back. With a momentary lapse in her memory, she moves over, leaves a space and whispers, "Is Peter coming?"

No—this gaping space at my side remains just that—gaping.
"Do you take this man to fill your space?"
"I do."
I glance about. All spaces are filled but mine.

I cry, "It is not good for woman to be alone—
to have a gaping space."

"In that day," declares the LORD, "you will call me 'my husband'" (Hosea 2:16).

Sunday, July 17

The house is darker now that summer is here and the trees are in full
foliage. Frost described the woods as "lovely, dark and deep." These
woods were all of that until the new owner next door decided to
uproot three acres of the lovely trees to plant another peach orchard.
That was a sad day.

But the trees on our acre still stand. They're protection—constant, unmoving, steadfast, like soldiers protecting a fort or like the
angels of the Lord encamped around those who fear him (Psalm
34:7). When I drive into the yard within the shelter of the trees, I
feel safe; I sense arms reaching out to me. It's like coming home to
loyal friends. We know the trees. We know which ones sprout their
leaves first in spring, which one last—the sunburst locust. We know
which maple dons gold in fall, which prefers orange and red. We
marvel at the cerise colour the oak chooses as its garb.

But the woods are strangely silent this summer. The spaces
between the trees are hollow with his absence.

Peter cut the big oak tree down in front of our yard. He came
into the house one day with one of his typical bombshell statements:
"The great oak has to fall."

With consternation I asked, "Which one?"

"The one by the road." (The only "great oak" left!)

"Don't be ridiculous! It's the most beautiful tree we have!"

"It's preventing the smaller oaks from growing."

"You can't cut down a beautiful, healthy tree for that reason."

"It has to go. The little ones can't grow in the shade of that big
tree."

"You can't! It's in its prime!"

"It has to go."

The symbolic meaning struck; I turned away with a burning behind my eyes.

The oak fell, exposing its great heart, the circling of its years. It fell not where Peter had planned and some of the little oaks were damaged in its fall.

Saturday, July 23

Ticking off the days–trying to make them manageable. Feeling lonely, tired, blue, listless. The ache of loss sinks deeper and deeper. I'm mourning the loss of summer holidays with Peter–trips from coast to coast, north and south; long lazy days at the lake, bicycle rides, outings, camping.

I sit on a beach nearby, stare across the water at a sunburned sky, and softly ask, *Where are you, Hon? It's been so long. I miss you so.*

A dip in the graph. Hanging in and bravely going through each day. Someone said I was brave to have Peter's picture hanging in the living room. Good grief!

"I thought about the former days, the years of long ago; I remembered my songs in the night" (Psalm 77:5,6).

The work of detaching myself from you
is becoming excruciatingly painful.
Then there's the task to somehow
navigate my world without your presence.
In addition to that, I need to redirect
my emotional energies to other people
and things in order to fill the void.
I'm tired. I hate my work.
I'd like to quit this job.
But–there are no U.I. benefits.

Tuesday, July 26

Must record this as a dark day. A sinister gloom hangs over all. It's impossible; I'll never, never, see his smile again. Loneliness feels like an ugly sore that refuses to heal.

I accompany Ruth Anne to another craft show—help a bit, wander around, listless. Everything seems so completely useless. Why make all this stuff? So utterly senseless to have one more thing to hang on a wall, set on a shelf, clutter a closet.

Nine months. Have done this now for nine long months. It's enough. Can't carry this grief any longer. I don't have any more tears. My heart feels like lead.

Have the dreadful feeling I could collapse. Misspelled my name on a card. Stared at it and couldn't remember. Yesterday, I got lost on my way to work.

Ruth Anne says it sounds like depression. Right. Kübler-Ross' next stage.

Nine months—gestation time for new birth. Will I ever leave this dark womb of grief and be born to light?

"...and my soul refused to be comforted" (Psalm 77:2).

A flood of memories engulfing, choking, blinding.
To place one foot before the other is sheer torture today.
I'd just as soon not bother. Restructure,
restructure your life they say. Pick up the pieces,
build something new. But I have no energy to sort
through the rubble to consider anything
let alone anything new.
This pain is exhausting, depleting,
draining me for today.
Will there come another day?

Wednesday, July 27

Sorting through the rubble. I remember Peter sorting through a heap of rubble–the chimney bricks from the house he tore down. He wanted to use them to build a wall in our basement behind a wood-burning stove. He chipped off the old mortar and gathered the best of the bricks in a pile. He started to lay them on a beautiful sunny day when I wanted to relax–go for a bike ride, out for lunch, enjoy the day together. He said he couldn't go; he had to build the wall. I went downstairs to ask again. Three rows of bricks were up– three rows of rather crooked bricks.

"Hon, get someone to do this for you. You've never laid bricks before," I said.

"No, I can do this. Come hold this string so I can fasten it on this end."

"It still sags. You need a bricklayer!"

I begged him to stop working, to relax, spend time together.

"Not today."

I left, upset, pedalled to Niagara, sipped a cup of coffee on a park bench, and wondered how much time we still would have together. Around 4 o'clock, calmed down, I returned. The wall was now mantel height.

"I've found a beautiful beam from the old house for a mantel."

I noticed the interesting whorls and grooves along the grain of the dark aged beam.

"I need your help to hold it so I can mortar bricks on top."

I held the beam. Peter smeared it with mortar and squished bricks into the soft mixture. Some oozed out like Pablum out of our babies' mouths.

"I think I have enough bricks to build a little wall as a woodbox partition and maybe enough to lay flat on the floor. And I want to take some of the old planks to build bookshelves.

"I'd like that, Hon; that will be nice."

I get a warm, loving feeling each time I go downstairs now and see that wall. It's not so crooked after all and the irregularities remind me so much of Peter. He sorted through the broken, the rubble, and built something new. It's an encouragement for me to follow.

Friday, July 29

The shaded deck is my refuge. The trees seem to wrap me in their silent darkness, allowing me mine. As they shadow the house, the yard, they seem to encourage me to keep travelling through this dark tunnel I'm in. It's the only way to emerge on the other side. And just as the trees will shed their leaves and let in more light, so my grief will be shed bit by bit and light will enter again. Hopefully. Hang in. "Your Father is as near when you journey through the dark tunnel as when under the open heaven!" (Cowman).

10

August

Last summer:

Peter called for me to come outside, "Come see what I did." I followed him to the end of the driveway. He'd been busy rebuilding the culvert using the foundation stones of the little house. He'd cemented them all nicely together.

"Can you see what I did?" he asked triumphantly.

My eyes wandered over the stones; I noticed a name written in the cement. And another. "Find them all," he said, "I wrote all of our names."

It took awhile; I counted on my fingers.

"One more, find the last one!"

His face shone with delight. His family—engraved on his heart, engraved on stone.

"See, I have engraved you on the palms of my hands" (Isaiah 49:16).

Tuesday, August 2

The prayer diary is still a source of strength and blessing. Yesterday:

"Jesus my Redeemer lives!

I, too, unto life must waken" (Moravian Text).

I've dwelt in death so long. I must waken and live. But it's so painful and there's no energy. I'm still so deep into this vale of tears.

Friday, August 12

Some of the heaviness has lifted. Am I finally approaching "Acceptance"? Is the circling of grief stretching to admit this state of being? I seem to be submitting more, resisting less, and finding new strength in the accompanying peace. The frightening feeling of not being able to make it has lessened. A certain measure of happiness dwells within. I don't dread going home. I don't dread the weekend, knowing I'll find something to do. It's three steps forward and two steps back. That was one of Peter's favourite school jokes:

"Why are you late?" the teacher asked.

"It was so slippery, every time I took two steps forwards, I slid three steps back."

"If that were true, how did you manage to arrive here?"

"I turned around and walked back home."

I've come out of these weeks of depression with a more trusting attitude that somehow I can make it being single. I'm more able to leave the matter of the future with the Lord. He'll braid it together somehow.

Is depression the deepest part of grief? Is that where we go when we grapple deep within with the reality that we must lay to rest the old in order for the new to begin? Is that the most difficult step? And does the body shut down in order for the spirit to "work" this through? I've read that those who refuse to travel through the depression "stage" of grief don't reach the same measure of healing as others do. But then, we all grieve differently and at our own pace.

~*Prayer Diary*:

Catherine's prayer: "I too long for a human companion with whom to share dreams and meaningful experiences. I entrust this desire to you."

Monday, August 23

I get the car licence changed to my name. Another erasure and, strangely, another jab of pain. The girl is quick and efficient. She understands. She makes no fuss that I forgot to even *bring* the licence! Bless her.

And so gradually he and everything about him and from him will pass, "and its place remembers it no more" (Psalm 103:16). Maybe make a scrapbook. Something tangible we can leaf through to remind us of all he was. Hold his memory. Tomorrow is his birthday.

"He will cover you with his feathers, and under his wings you will find refuge" (Psalm 91:4).

11

September

The desert is slowly changing, or is the change within me? It seems not so arid and dry. The terrain is easier. There's more life within and around. The well of tears is drying up, and there's more joy as I walk through my day.

> *I've reached a place of healing at the Master's feet*
> *and wonder who transported me*
> *as I was weak and could not walk.*
> *I look and see four friends still standing*
> *by the stretcher on which they carried me.*
> *I smile my grateful thanks.*
> *"Get up and live," the Master says to me.*
> *"Well done," He says to them,*
> *"Your work will be rewarded."*

Monday, September 12

I've always resisted having a quiet time in the morning, but now I treasure the hour I spend reading, thinking, writing, praying. The longer I have, the better. It's a time to touch base with myself, with

God. Time to reflect where I am, what hurts, as in everything just now, as this day last year was the beginning of our holiday in Australia.

"When I said, 'My foot is slipping,' your love, O LORD, supported me. When anxiety was great within me, your consolation brought joy to my soul" (Psalm 94:18,19).

Tuesday, September 13

Our wedding anniversary—pain of all pains. The children sent flowers. Still amazed how much worse it is on a special day. I go to work, smile, keep busy the rest of the day with telephone calls and visits. I can't let myself become fully aware of what was lost lest it overwhelm me.

~*Prayer Diary*:
Peter's note:

At the Parkway for our 28th wedding anniversary. Dined on steak and crab. Had a great weekend. Soaked in the Jacuzzis.

A bittersweet reminder of what used to be.

Wednesday, September 14

Not a good idea not to cry yesterday. I arrive at work this morning and "How are you?" triggers the tears. Grief wells up like a strong tide and I can't hold it back, can't hold it together, can't summon up the "strong lady" who lives within somewhere. I need to take the day off.

Leave your grief at home. Don't bring it to work.

I know by now what to do: sit by the lake; have a cup of coffee. Be with the pain; it will pass. Trust the process; it moves forward. Tomorrow I'll feel stronger. I'm moving forward. And I'll remind myself that "Sorrows come to stretch out spaces in the heart for joy." Spaces where empathy and understanding dwell, for me to give, for others to draw from.

Gibran puts it this way: "The deeper sorrow carves into your being, the more joy you can contain."

As the tide rushes in so comes my grief.
It sweeps over me in waves of tears and sadness
and intense longing for his presence.
I experience the pain,
let it wash over me
in all its stinging force.
It gradually recedes,
flows back into the ocean,
and I get up, blink in the sunlight
and deeply breathe in life.
I wonder when the next tide is due.

Saturday, September 17

Nine singles come to my house for a potluck dinner tonight. We met at the fall singles' conference last weekend and want to keep in touch. We whined a lot about couples not inviting us over, so we decided to reach back to when we were young and not married. Then we didn't complain about couples leaving us out. We provided our own fun. Make springs for yourselves in the desert!

We play Pictionary, and hilarity fills the room. We place an easel of sorts on the mantel so everyone can see our nervous efforts at drawing. We talk and joke and could pass for a group of giddy teenagers. I'm astonished to hear my own hearty laughter. My face is turned toward life and living tonight. Maybe I'm leaving my "mourning bench" for longer periods of time. Maybe eventually I'll sit on it only a few times each year.

"Praise the LORD...who satisfies...so that your youth is renewed like the eagle's" (Psalm 103:2,5).

Saturday, September 24

I hike up and down the escarpment alone and sit on a rock to admire the goldenrod and the magentas. Fall–Peter's favourite time of the year. I hear him recite the poem: "The goldenrod is yellow, the corn is turning brown."

This is the first fall he's missing. Is he really missing it?

While driving home, the setting sun is directly ahead. Trees line the road and create a long golden tunnel with the magnificent bright light at the end.

Everything in life fades in comparison to that glorious light at the end of the road.

12

October

October—nostalgic month dressed in flame and gold.
When the leaves are falling,
I will remember
it was fall when you fell.
The memory is with me all day; it surrounds me like the leaves on the yard. Nearly a year. There seems to be such a distortion in time. Where was I all year? Plodding alongside grief as it marched through the desert?

Now it's as if I'm climbing a difficult hill, and it'll take to the end of the month to reach the top. And I'm tired. I make another appointment with my grief counsellor. He reminds me there's a peak in the process at the end of the first year.

Monday, October 10

Will these "firsts" ever stop? It's Thanksgiving Day. A day Peter always made so special with a hike on the Bruce Trail, cooking the turkey, laughter…

It's a wet blustery day, and I seem to be so deeply back into grief. "It sounds like it'll be one day at a time again, Mom," the children remind me. And so, we get through the day.

We go for our hike in spite of the wind and rain. Josh and I hold hands as we slither up a hill on the Bruce Trail.

"We'll make it, right Grandma?"

"Yes, Josh, we'll make it."

Sunday, October 16

A friend takes me for a hike in the woods. There's something soothing about being among trees—the softness of the leaf-strewn path, the sprinkling of light through the protective colourful canopy. We come out into a clearing. One lone tree in full golden foliage stands centre stage. It's grandeur is breathtaking. The sun comes out from behind the clouds and transforms the tree into a magnificent golden sphere. I'm overwhelmed to see this beauty and at night sit down to write:

> *A tree decked out*
> *in autumn's blazing glory*
> *caught my eye and held me still.*
> *It stood so tall,*
> *alone,*
> *midst others green, grey*
> *and shrivelled brown.*
> *The Sun came out*
> *and shone upon that tree*
> *and in that Light it was transformed*
> *from glory into glory.*
> *I beheld and wistfully gave thanks—*
> *for you.*

I decide this will be my memorial to Peter to be printed in the local paper on the 27th.

Tuesday, October 25

A few more days and this year in the desert will be over. I feel a readiness to go on. We've discussed finishing the basement and I feel ready now to tackle it. Even a few weeks ago the thought would've overwhelmed me.

Life will take on a pattern: work, family, friends, new friends. It seems as if I've been on a merry-go-round all year, going in circles. I'm more or less ready now to step off and join the mainstream again. It will mean trying to fit in alone. The special status of "newly bereaved" will be gone. The W on my forehead has faded.

What of the desert image? Have I arrived now among trees and shade? It's more a sense that I'm back, that I've joined the rest again.

This day last year may well have been one of the happiest days of my life—a most gracious gift.

"He heals the brokenhearted and binds up their wounds" (Psalm 147:3).

Thursday, October 27

Did most of my crying yesterday and that helps to live today—the first anniversary. Family, friends, flowers, phone calls. Everyone is so thoughtful. We visit the cemetery to see the stone, finally in place. The inscription reads: *Because I live, you will live also* (John 14:19, NKJV). Peter wrote this three times one day in the prayer diary—heavily underlined it. I see the multiple meaning.

We go out for supper and then call Jim and Julie to tell them I'm planning a trip back to Australia some time early next year. I've been corresponding with Margaret, the social worker, and she's invited me to stay at her place while in Alice Springs.

All of Peter's family drops in for the evening at my invitation. I show some of Peter's slides from our trip a year ago and Ruth Anne reads the poem that summarizes it all. The family expresses how good it is to be together, to remember.

One of the children says, "I feel lighter. It's as if something has lifted."

Another comments, "Your second year will be easier, Mom, because you did so much work during this first year." I hope that is true, although I hear many find that during the second year they reach a still deeper level of grief. More pain. But the Lord "sustains the fatherless and the widow" (Psalm 146:9).

"As long as we have memories, yesterday will remain. As long as we have purpose, tomorrow will have hope."

~Prayer Diary:

Peter's note: *Thank more, rejoice more, laugh more, praise more, compliment more, be positive, be genuine.*

What a message to send along as I enter the second year!

Thanks, Hon. Reading the prayer diary this year, especially your notations in it, has been an amazing experience. You've left us so much. And even though the path ahead still looks daunting and difficult, with God's grace and help, we will go on.

Remembering, One Year Later

You scaled a mountaintop
before you left your home
and watched a glowing sun
sink in the western sky,
never to see it again.
You frolicked on red rocks,
played with a snake in sand,
spread our lunch upon a tree
felled, as you would shortly be.
You drank it in,
the rugged beauty all around,
and savoured every bit.

You scaled the heights of human touch
as laughter and kind words
flowed from your lips
to those both far and near.
Your enjoyment knew no bounds
at seeing beads and pelts
and heat-burned wood
and people of a different skin.
A height of inner joy was also reached
as you communed with Him
and shared with us His word.
A perfect peace enveloped you that day
as you received a glimpse of things to come—
a hint of heaven reflected on your face.

You scaled the heights—
and far below I watched,
marvelled and gave thanks.

Part IV

The Desert Revisited

1989

*"Be at rest once more, O my soul, for
the* LORD *has been good to you"*
(Psalm 116:7).

1

G'day Again

The aircraft banks sharply and descends for the landing. We're warmly welcomed to Cairns airport with the usual cheery "G'day" by the staff–the men smartly dressed in Bermuda shorts. I look around and spot Jim and Dylan walking toward me. Dylan's blue eyes smile readily and I pick him up for hugs and kisses. I ruffle his gorgeous white curls.

We walk out of the terminal into sunshine, plants, flowers and bird calls. I'm back.

Jim takes the road north marked *To the beaches.* A string of beaches lies north of Cairns and each connects to the highway by a separate road, much like the teeth of a comb or the tines of a fork. Palm Cove, where Jim and Julie lived last year, is the last of "the beaches." Today, Jim swings onto the second-to-last road, which leads to the small town of Kewarra with its stretch of beach.

We turn into a new subdivision and then onto the paved drive of their just-completed home. The house stands out among the others on the street because Jim, the plant lover, has landscaped it lavishly with palms, shrubs and tropical plants. Julie and two-month-old Chrissie are waiting for us. I gently hug and kiss another gorgeous blue-eyed grandchild. Peter's gold coin is hers.

213

"Go walk, Gramma?" Dylan asks after supper. He has quite a vocabulary for a twenty-month-old.

"I'd love to," I say.

He takes my hand as if I'm a well-known friend and we walk along the edge of the backyard lawn.

"This frangipani," he says, pointing to a small fragrantly blooming shrub. "Smell." I bend close and inhale the strong fragrance of the pure white blossom. "Oh, this smells so lovely." Dylan is pleased. So is Jim, sitting on the patio. Dylan points to other plants, recites the names as he remembers them.

"Careful, owie plant," he says, sidestepping a patch of lawn. We bend down to examine the small green paddle-like leaves and I touch them. They sting a bit as they grip my finger.

Jim laughs, "He's very careful when he's barefoot not to step on the "owie plant."

We spend the evening on the patio. It's good to be back.

Tuesday, January 31

The sunshine alone is worth it! We spend a quiet day reconnecting, enjoying each other's company.

I'm anxious to explore the beach and enjoy some time alone. I walk down the road to where it ends at a large resort by the beach. The resort's bamboo exterior and thatched roof blend with the strip of forest left standing here. The undergrowth is thick, except along the resort where they've cleared the brush away and formed winding pebble paths underneath white-mottled trees. I take one of the paths and emerge to see the beautiful crescent beach again! The deep hue of the Coral Sea is just as I remember it–an aquamarine sparkling jewel.

Peter and I passed here on a Sunday afternoon hike from Trinity Beach back to Palm Cove. We didn't even see the resort through the trees. It's barely visible. It must've been here that we saw a lone man emerge from the trees. We said, "G'day," but he was sullen and didn't return our greeting.

I can see Palm Cove's jetty jut out into the water far to my left. I'm sure we'll drive up to the cove one day.

2

Not So Good a Day

Thursday, February 2

I take my book to the beach this afternoon while everyone naps. I walk through the enchanted forest on one of the pebble paths beside the resort and exult in the lovely never-ending view of the sea. A couple is sunbathing to my left; a family with two little children are playing to the right. No one else is here. I spread my towel between the two parties, lie down facing the water and become engrossed in my novel.

Time is irrelevant. I don't hear the family leave. I don't hear the couple leave. I'm totally unaware of my surroundings.

Suddenly–thud!

Something pounces. An animal? A man!

Stunned and shocked, strength curses through me like lightning. I struggle. *Must get on my feet.*

Desperately I fight, finally stand, and face my assailant eye to eye. "Don't you dare touch me!" I spit out the angry words.

We glare at each other, animal-like. He's young, muscular, blond, hands raised, eyes blazing.

He takes a step; I spring back. Another step; I spring back again, every muscle wound like a corkscrew. My feet are in the water. With one quick glance I scoop up the scene. *No one else on the beach...backed up into the water…he can outrun me…outwrestle me…screaming will anger him…no one might hear me…my purse…he's between me and my purse…*

I'm totally defenceless. A wave of sheer terror grabs my gut.

Oh, Lord!

Something happens. There's a change. His eyes lose their glare; his hands drop to his sides; his jaw relaxes. He's only a youth. He stands silent. Then mutters, "I'm sorry I frightened you."

He turns around and walks away, past my purse, into the trees.

Every muscle trembles. I can't move. I wait until he's out of sight, then shakily walk toward my things. I pick up my book, my towel, my purse and with rubbery legs navigate over the sand to one of the paths. Through the trees, I see the young man jump on an old red bicycle and ride away. I wait until he's out of sight again.

I'm shaking so. *Best go into the resort. Need to report this.* I walk into the spacious, airy bamboo lobby. Fans whir overhead. Three beautiful young women stand behind a polished dark wooden counter. *Which one to approach?*

Shaking too much…have to sit down.

The lobby fills. A busload of tourists has arrived. Everyone is greeted warmly. Smiling waiters walk around carrying trays filled with small glasses of pink punch topped with festive little umbrellas. A grinning waiter hands me a drink. *I need to report. It'll upset this happy party. They won't believe me.*

Still shaking, I slowly make my way home. Jim's eyes moisten with concern. He dials the police. Two officers come and take down all the details. I try to give an accurate description of the man. They apologize profusely for this unfortunate incident. They're dismayed this has happened to one of Australia's tourists. They assure me it's an isolated incident. It won't happen again.

At night, I sit on the dark, quiet patio and sip my tea. It's so still, so peaceful. It seems incredible that something so dangerous happened today. But I'm safe. I was protected. What was the turning point? Why the change in the man? It was as if a film passed over his face. An angel wing?

It's the beginning of my stay here. Did God allow the incident as a timely warning? A wake-up call to the reality of my vulnerability as I travel alone? I'll heed the warning, be more vigilant, and not be found alone anywhere on this trip.

3

Better Days

I decide to pedal to Palm Cove. It's hot, but the car is still in the repair shop, and the bicycle ride turns out to be enjoyable with little traffic on the road. A right turn on the last "tine of the fork" will take me to this idyllic coastal town hidden among trees. I cycle past Jim and Julie's old house, see the beautiful bougainvillea.

At the cove's beach, I lean the bike against a palm tree. It's all the same—the beach, Double Island, the colourful shops, the Tea House nestled among the trees. More of the forest has been cut back to accommodate a large new hotel tucked behind the Tea House.

I wander and remember. Memories come not fast and furious but gently and tenderly. I see everything through the eyes of a year later. I'm at a different place.

I stroll on the soft sand and remember the footprints we made. The lonely palm still stands at the far right—monument to my Waterloo. Tears well up. I see the fearful, struggling woman crying so desperately—the year-ago I. If I'd trusted more, I wouldn't have been so consumed with fear. I want to speak to her—words well up to comfort her:

Don't be so afraid. Your Father will be very gentle with you. He'll arrange for you to have the most beautiful days together, to part with your love intact. He has planned for strangers to look after you. He has instructed them all. *Hear Him say to you, "Fear not, my daughter. I am your Father and I care for you more deeply than you can even imagine. Trust in me, rest in me. I AM in charge."*

I sit on the sand, listen to the waves as they lick the shore. Words drift in to describe this day.

A ribbon of soft white sand
runs along the ocean's edge;
waves play a game of tag.
Hills dressed in luscious green
watch over the peaceful scene;
birds sing and laugh.
A strange contentment washes
over me on this solitary path.
It's a feeling
It's a knowing
I've done battle with a raging sea—
I've survived
I've arrived
at a place of peace.

Saturday, February 11

A sleepless night. I go for an early morning walk to have a private cry. What will I find in Alice Springs? Will all the pain come back in full force? Will I find healing? Closure? I've been so lethargic. Maybe it's the heat. I'm marking time—waiting for ten days to pass before I go to Alice. Maybe I need the rest before my journey back. Sounds so much like sixteen months ago.

Leafing through the Book of Psalms—the message is constantly the same: He loves, is compassionate, a refuge, will guide, lead, satisfy your desires; trust, commit, don't fret, hope in Him. Can I use this part of my journey to learn more—to develop a closer walk with God?

Lord, help me to experience the "shelter of Your presence" as I journey back and, in that shelter, learn of You.

Sunday, February 12

I bike to Trinity Beach and walk the trail to the land head. A beautiful scenic view. So I sit here and ponder. I've been here two weeks, have only had two crying spells. Peter is so far away. I'm involved in life, the present, and a future that does not include him. I'm content to mosey around by myself. I feel good about the independence–being able to take care of myself. Am I just suppressing, or am I truly healing? It's almost strange to feel happy and light-hearted today, to really enjoy the bike ride alone. But then, I'm a part of family here. There are loved ones waiting when I return home today. I'd feel differently coming to an empty house. I'd pray for angels.

I called Ruth Anne this morning. Her baby is due any day. Spoke to Josh. He said, "Now how are things down there, Grandma? Have you seen a kangaroo and have you seen a koala bear?"

Tuesday, February 14

Valentine's Day, again. Last year was so difficult, walking alone in the morning, buying that rose. Today–completely different. I'm so glad the year of "firsts" has passed. There was a card from Josh and Kaleb in yesterday's mail and there's one from Dylan and Chrissie at the breakfast table.

> *Dear Grandma,*
>   *We are so glad you could visit us awhile 'cause we love your soft voice and especially your smile. I (Dylan) love to read my books with you, and you don't even mind cleaning up my poo! I love the time we spend on our walks, and I (Chrissie) love to smile at your "baby talk." Daddy wants to celebrate with a beer 'cause he hasn't had to do dishes since you've been here, and Mommy is so happy 'cause now she has someone with whom to "extrovert." I guess what we are really trying to say is, we hope you have a Happy Valentine's Day. We love you! Dylan and Chrissie xxxx*

Wednesday, February 15

I'm taking a sightseeing tour today. The bus picks me up at the Kewarra Resort and drives to Cairns. There we catch the little tourist train up into the hills to Kuranda. Peter and I were going to do this. *Well, I'm still getting to do it, Hon, and I'm enjoying it.*

I find a travelling companion in a girl from Brisbane who is venturing out on her own for the first time. We stop in Atherton for lunch and a visit to a tea plantation. We drive on to see waterfalls, a dam, a crater, and have a cruise on Lake Barrine. We climb 3000 ft. to the Great Divide. Then a hair-raising descent of 2000 ft. within twelve kilometres with 247 hairpin turns through the trees. In one of the turns, we see something that looks very much like a "lady of the woods" waiting to catch a ride. It's a bikini painted on a tree! The bus driver dryly tells us that she's had a breast enlargement recently and someone gave her a new bikini.

Back in town, the bus driver drops his passengers off at their respective locations. Then he drives to Kewarra and asks me which road. He turns in and drops me off at Jim's front door! I'm safe.

Saturday, February 18

When I return from the Trinity Beach pool this afternoon, Jim says, "How many grandchildren did you say you have?" Ruth Anne called. She has delivered a beautiful dark-haired, brown-eyed baby girl! We're ecstatic. I'm torn—needing to be here, wanting to be there. Her name is Leah Angelina! I'm so honoured to be part of her name!

After supper, I go for a walk and shed the expected tears. Peter's not here to welcome another granddaughter. The ache of it overwhelms me.

Sunday, February 19

In a dream, Peter totally ignored me. I was upset and told him I didn't know what was going on. Was he alive or dead? We'd had a funeral service and a memorial service, so that must mean he's dead. I looked at him and said, "It has to be one way or the other. If you're dead, then please be gone. If you're alive, then please stay. I can't take the torture of not knowing."

It sounds as if I want to be done. I feel bad that the dream left me with such a negative feeling. He wasn't nice and loving like in all the other dreams. I was impatient for him to go and not keep torturing me.

Maybe that's what grief really is: torture. Hanging on, yet knowing there's no substance; and the hanging on becomes more torturous than the letting go. With the letting go, there is at least freedom to move ahead.

4

Alice Springs

Tuesday, February 21

I spend some quiet time alone early this morning to garner courage for this trip back to Alice. I'm feeling apprehensive and somewhat sad. Here I am doing the difficult; yet it's part of the journey I want to take. But how will it go?

Peter jotted Psalm 5:1-5 in the prayer diary at yesterday's date, so I look up the verses.

> *Give ear to my words, O LORD, consider my sighing.*
> *Listen to my cry for help, My King and my God, for to you I pray.*
> *In the morning, O LORD, you hear my voice; in the morning I lay*
> *my requests before you and wait in expectation* (vs. 1-3).

Jim takes me to the airport after supper. Our words are few; he wishes me well. I board and the plane climbs swiftly to scale the sharp rise of hills beyond which lie the lush, fertile Atherthon Tablelands. Then the outback—the endless stretch of sandy red earth, its colour deepened by the setting sun. The *Never-Never.*

I fight back tears as I glimpse twinkling lights—Alice, huddled in the curve of the mountain's shadowed spine. The City of Light. I stifle a dry shuddering sob as I step into the warm night air and walk toward the terminal. Margaret is waiting and we reach out to each other with a hug.

"I wondered whether I'd recognize you," she says.

"I wondered the same thing!" I say.

She drives to her house across the dry topsy-turvy Todd and we chit-chat over a cup of tea before she shows me to my room.

What awaits me? I haven't gone this way before.

Wednesday, February 22

I go through some of my journal written a year ago and release some pent-up tears. The Uniting Church bulletin from last year's service with Psalm 128 written on it is tucked between the pages of my journal. I read the psalm again and suddenly see the words "may you live to see your children's children" in a different light. I've focused on the fact that Peter did *not* get to see his grandchild Daniel as he felt he was promised. Now I see that he *did* live to see his grandchildren. He lived to see three of them!

All the words in the psalm are true of him. It's like a picture, a summary of his life. He was blessed because he feared the Lord. The fruit of his labour: his career, the farm, the new house, the love of people at school, at church. Blessings and prosperity. His wife: a fruitful vine–certainly! Sons like olive shoots around our table. I think of a photo of Peter with our four tall, strapping, handsome sons. He *was* blessed and lived to see his children's children!

At 11 o'clock, I decide to walk to town, retrace my steps. It's hot. Margaret told me it would be 40° C. "It doesn't go beyond 40° C in summer," she laughed. "We keep it there lest the tourists panic."

"You mean they don't report anything higher?"

"That's right," she chuckled.

I walk on the familiar sidewalks, past the grand old hotel, past the shops. I enter the Ford Plaza. The splash of the fountain greets me, the hum of air conditioners and conversation, the click of heels, the slap of flip-flops. The greenery still cascades down; light beams through the windows.

I have a cup of coffee in the cafeteria. A couple is sitting in the chairs Peter and I sat in after he bought his kangaroo skin. I wander through the mall, the gift shop, the kiosk.

It takes a good half hour to walk down Larapinta Drive to the Stuart Caravan Park. I go through the gate and avoid looking toward the office, as I don't want to talk to anyone or explain my presence. Which path was it? I remember the rising sun, so I wander under the trees toward the east side of the park. It's like a wooded garden, so still, so serene. Only a few caravans stand here and there.

I find our site. The space is deserted. Good. No campers close by. A log lies across a shortcut we took to reach our camper. It's as if the site has been cordoned off. It's holy ground. I lower myself on the row of logs that surrounds the site; I inhale the scene, suspended in time, dabbing my eyes.

Somehow, it's good to be back. The shade of the large fine-leaved tree overhead covers me. It's only a campsite, yet we lived here. We drank of life and love more deeply maybe than ever before, despite the threat of death. Peter's feet padded across this sand as he made his way to the shower in the middle of the night while I slept. I'm glad he made it back to the camper.

The sky is intensely blue beyond the trees; its brightness stings my eyes. Heaven opened here to welcome a soul, a blessed soul. The most joyful event for him, the most devastating for me. His Day. My Night.

There's a strong sense the former overrides the latter. It's an awesome thing to walk with someone right to heaven's vestibule, as it were, where unseen angels hover. "And bring each other Home," Claudia sang. I was privileged to be with him here, on this spot, where he approached the Light, where he was born to Life.

The tears are now dripping from my jawline as if from a leaky faucet. Fifty-five years his heart beat, then stuttered and stalled. Earthly life ended but eternal life began. How can I fathom it all?

I continue to sit in silence—don't want to leave this peaceful, hallowed spot.

A sentence forms: "There's a plot of land on Larapinta Drive in the town of Alice Springs." Bits of rhythmic joy skip across the strand of words. There's so much in my heart; maybe these words are bubbling up as a way to sum it all up.

I walk back into town to the beat of emerging phrases.

I have numerous questions to ask Margaret when she returns home from her work at the hospital.

"How was it you had all day to spend with me?" is uppermost.

She smiles. "We're set up that way. You're not the first to lose a loved one out here in the desert. The hospital is prepared to care for the family members. They have two social workers on staff."

She tells me many of these family members have stayed in her home as guests while they planned how to proceed.

"Remember, I invited you to stay at my place?" she asks.

"Yes, I do remember."

"I would've loved to have had you stay with me."

"I was so anxious to get to Adelaide. And you were able to get it all arranged," I say gratefully.

"You made such an impression on me," she says. "I watched you go through that day and knew the Lord was with you. I just wanted to gather you up and soothe away all the pain I could see in you."

"Oh, thank you, Margaret. You made such an impression on *me* that day! Your poster of the koala bear and the caption *Relax, I AM in charge.* It's the first thing I noticed when I entered your office, and that made me think you also knew the Shepherd."

"For sure."

"What about the young girl, Michelle, who stayed with me at first? Who was she?"

"I thought it a bit of a miracle that she was there," Margaret replies. "She's a nurse who worked in *casualty*. She'd been called to come in for a special case; then you came, and they asked if she'd look after you. They knew of her expertise dealing with crises. And she also knows the Shepherd, as you put it. When I saw Michelle was with you, I realized God had His hand in the events of that day."

"She was terrific. Is she still here?"

"No, I'm sorry, she's gone to work somewhere else."

"A man came to the campsite shortly after the ambulances. He said he had come to look after me. Do you have any idea who that might've been? I remember how when I first saw him I thought he was an angel because all I could see was his glistening white shirt."

She ponders a moment and looks blank. "I guess the only one it could have been is Steve Peers, operations manager of St. John's Ambulance here in Alice. He often takes it upon himself to follow the ambulances in his own car to see whether family members need assistance."

"He was amazing. I would've gone into terrible shock had he not come."

"I'm glad someone was there for you at that moment."

"I'm so impressed," I say softly. "I felt so cared for—felt as if God had all of you in place that day."

"I'm glad you felt cared for. I think we here in the desert are very conscious of how much we depend on each other for survival. So we do our best."

We continue our visit. Margaret tells me about the many years she has spent in the outback working with a church organization to help the Aborigines.

"I've attempted to bake biscuits with flour that was literally walking towards me."

"Pardon?" I gulp.

"Bugs, worms. You could see the flour move," she explains.

I shudder.

"I've been in situations where I've had one billy can of water to wash my face or to quench my thirst," she continues and tells me more of her experiences.

I comment gratefully, "Your 'cup of water' was the greatest gift to me that day, Margaret. I'll never forget it."

Thursday, February 23

I hear Margaret leave for work and at once am overwhelmed with emotion. I sit at the kitchen table and try to eat some breakfast. The poem that began to form yesterday comes to me verse after verse as if it were already written. It sounds like a ballad of sorts. At noon Margaret comes home. I hadn't expected her and feel a little embarrassed about the state I'm in.

"It's OK," she says, "I know you have a lot to work through."

"I'll be all right. I've written most of it down. That always helps."

I offer to cook *tea* tonight.

The poem begs a conclusion. How can I sum up his life? The meaning of it?

A memory flickers. I'm back in the farmhouse, at the kitchen sink, washing dishes. Eleven-year-old Wayne is drying them. Our Bible memory booklets stand propped open on the windowsill, and we repeat lines from Micah 6:8. "And what does the LORD require of you? To act justly and to love mercy and to walk humbly with your God."

"Imagine, Wayne," I say, "just three things: act justly, love mercy, walk humbly. That's all God asks of us in order to live a good life."

He looks at me, his impish grin lighting up his face.

I write the last verse of the poem and walk into town to buy spaghetti and sauce.

Friday, February 24

I'm taking a bus tour of Alice at 2 o'clock. We stop at the telegraph station and the spring, the Flying Doctor's headquarters, Anzac Hill; it's all familiar; it's good to see it again.

I'm thankful I'm able to be back. The town holds so much meaning. The happiest days, the saddest day—all in one place; yet the overtone is peace. I have no quarrel with Alice.

The perspective is completely different than sixteen months ago. The death scene was vivid for so long at the beginning. Often I wished it could be erased. Yet, yesterday at the caravan park, I could see beyond the scene. I could see the whole picture—the before, the present, the after—and that diminished, almost eradicated, the sting of the scene.

The bus stops at Guth's Art Gallery.

A 20 x 200 ft. panorama by Henk Guth of the central Australian landscape is housed in a circular building. We climb the stairs to the viewing level. The painted canvas encircles us. It is truly a work of art. We slowly walk around the protective railing to see all of it—a lonely outback landscape alight with colour, dotted with pale greenery. A dry creek bed curls among rocks and a line of trees; shadowy mountains rise in the distance, fade into the horizon.

Reproductions of details of the grand scene are available. I descend the stairs to the shop and buy a print of a clump of white ghost gums. It's a tiny fragment of the whole. I climb the stairs again to see where this clump of trees fits into the total picture. *Oh, there they are!*

To see the pale quartet of trees alone on a sheet of paper or to see them as part of the complete panorama offers a completely different perspective. By themselves, the trees are the central focus on the page. I notice the smooth curve of the silken white trunks contrasted by some dark shrubs behind, the soft yellow-green of the leaves, a fallen branch, pink on the red earth.

There's a different message in the whole of the vista. The particulars of the clump of trees fade but I find them so tastefully blended into the landscape, their position so fitting beside the dry riverbed.

It reminds me how different my perspective is sixteen months after Peter's death. Alive, he was a strong immediate presence, so commanding I could hardly remember him as a younger man. Now that he's gone, I'm more able to see the total picture. I see all of him: how he was at different stages, how he changed, grew. And I see more clearly how our landscape was enriched by his presence, just as this clump of trees adds dimension to and enhances this work of art. Peter's brushstroke on our lives was broad. His joy coloured our world like the pinkish tones washed over Guth's masterpiece.

Margaret and I enjoy the evening together. She tells me more.

"The staff met to discuss Peter's case. The doctors worked on him for over an hour to try to revive him."

"Yes, I remember the doctor telling me this. Afterwards I remembered I'd promised Peter I wouldn't let anyone try to revive him."

"The ambulance worker said she believed Peter was already gone when they arrived at the park."

"I've thought of it that way all along, but I'm glad to hear you say it. At times I've struggled with the thought that maybe he regained consciousness and called for me."

"No, he didn't."

The evening is still. Soft light glows from the centre of town. Margaret goes in to make us a cup of tea.

Sunday, February 26

I walk into the Uniting Church a little late for the morning service, not quite trusting myself to be able to do this. I find a seat in the back. *Peter in flip-flops, slapping up the aisle, Bible in hand, excited, anticipating...*

Dr. Vanclay speaks and saves the day—*Bless him, Lord.* Moses wanted answers, data, but all he received was I AM. Our questions aren't answered; we live with not knowing; but the great I AM is in control.

Monday, February 27

Heavy, sad day—sixteen months today. Still such swings from acceptance back to shocking pain. How often will this vast emptiness astonish me again? When I think I have somewhat arrived, I find myself again where I started.

> And the end of all our exploring
> Will be to arrive where we started
> And know the place for the first time (T. S. Eliot).

I spend the day wandering around town with that "haunting wistfulness" braided into every moment. I sit to have a cup of coffee where we sat together. I have lunch where we had lunch together. I walk up Anzac Hill once more, stop at the war memorial with the fat chain-link–remember him pensively asking the question, "What more do I want?" Is this where he truly understood he'd be leaving soon?

I sit on one of the benches and for a moment I'm back in that night so full of love and meaning. The gentle darkness settled around us, but he was aware of the light. "It's not over," he whispered. Just a slight turn of the head and–the "City of Light." The veil separating "here" and "hereafter" so sheer. And we had no words. Just a silent wonder and a holding of hands as in awe we descended our little mountain.

I wander around the small space, now suddenly dry and bare and empty. Empty of Peter. Tears well up.

It's been so long, Hon. I miss you so much today...

With tears now streaming down my face, I hear the words that would be audible were he here:

I loved you so much, and I love you now in a deeper, richer way. I follow your progress, feel your pain, and my joy knows no bounds when you succeed. Keep following our gracious Lord, for He loves you perfectly and cares for you so deeply. Entrust the rest of your journey to Him. I'm cheering for you. And when you arrive, we'll see each other face to face and you will know as you are known. We'll spend eternity enjoying a love beyond your wildest imagination. Hang in there, gal. Live!

5

Uluru

I decide since I'm here, I need to take the opportunity to visit Ayers Rock. The proper Aborigine name is *Uluru*, which means weeping, howling. It's a three-day adventure.

Our bus driver, an excellent tour guide, tells us about a lone rubber tree that grows in the outback—a freak of nature. We pepper him with questions. A rubber tree way out here in the outback? How can that be?

"You'll get a glimpse of it shortly," he reassures us.

Finally, we see a far-off tree. We stare at the distant shape that shortly sprouts limbs and a few dried leaves. And running shoes. Rubber shoes nailed to its trunk and to most of its branches!

"Now didn't I tell you it was a rubber tree?"

We've been taken; the bus rings with laughter.

At Yulara, a tourist "village" a few miles from the Rock, I book into a motel. At sunset we're taken by bus for our first close-up view of the Rock, and to watch this hump in the desert change colour as the last of the sun's rays paint it deeper and deeper shades of red and purple.

Back at the motel, a man, dark hair slicked back, passes me, stops, and observes where I enter. *He knows my room.* Panic rises.

I quickly slip inside, lock the door. It's secure. I cross the room to check the patio door. The screen has a lock, a tiny lever. It seems so flimsy. Anyone could force it. I close the large glass doors. The lock is jammed; it doesn't work. No matter how hard I try, it doesn't budge. I can't go back out alone to report this. I draw the drapes tightly shut. Keep checking the door.

At 2 o'clock I'm still awake.

Wednesday, March 1
6 a.m.

The bus takes us for a tour to Ayers Rock. Those who want to climb it must do so at this hour. The heat later on makes it too risky. A guide tells us how many have died of heart attacks. *And Peter insisted he'd do the climb.* The guide does his best to dissuade us, but I've decided and bravely start. It takes me an hour to climb to the top. *I'm doing it for you, Hon.* The view is out of this world, or rather, of the whole world—this empty red world. The rounded eroded boulders of Mount Olga are some kilometres away; the horizon is all around. On the way down, I chat with a man from Toronto. My legs are rubbery when I finally reach the desert floor again.

David and Amy, a couple from California whom I met on the bus yesterday, are waiting for me.

"We're rather worried about you," they say. "You looked so tired this morning."

They invite me to spend the rest of the day with them. We swim in the Sheraton pool and in the evening sit on the bar patio and listen to musicians sing love songs. Most of them have the same sad undercurrent: "I thought I'd see you once again."

I appreciate David and Amy, am touched by their concern for me. I see it as God's care after last night's scare. Our conversation is stimulating. They look to me for ideas about their work, their situation. So much of my focus has been on: *What do I need? Who is there for me?* It's time I begin to ask: *How can I be there for you?*

6

Waltzing Matilda

Friday, March 3

A bus tour to Glen Helen seems like an appropriate way to top off my ten-day voyage to the Red Centre. Our transport is a twelve-seater four-wheel drive Land Rover with red-haired, storytelling Dennis at the wheel. It's a jolly ride.

We stop to see Flynn's grave and then Simpson's Gap. I remember Peter trying to scramble to the other side. There's more water today—doubt whether he would've made it.

It's noon when we arrive at Standley Chasm—the one Peter and I didn't get to see. I stumble on stones in the narrow passage as I peer up at the sheer rock walls to a dizzying height of eighty metres above where a slice of blue sky separates them. It seems the walls may at any time close in on us, squash us like caterpillars. We stand silent, wait for the moment the sun will enter the thin strip of blue. It strikes and the quartzite rock leaps into colourful life. A glowing red spreads first down one wall and then the other, as if someone spilled cans of red paint over them. The walls act like sponges that absorb all the paint and momentarily they return to their usual shade of rust the moment the sun has passed.

We climb back into the rover and settle in for the long ride to Glen Helen, 135 kilometres from Alice. To our delight, Dennis tells tales of life outback, stories sprinkled with dry Australian humour. During a lull in the storytelling, he recites the whole saga of "The Man from Snowy River."

> There was movement at the station,
> for the word had passed around
> that the colt from old Regret had got away... (Paterson).

We're served a barbeque at Glen Helen and wander to the Fink River to see it flow through yet another gap in the mountain range.

On the way back I rest my head and, as the deserted red countryside slides past my window, I reflect on my days here. They were good days despite the pain and tears. They were necessary days—gathering the pieces, remembering, mourning, finding meaning, letting go.

The lonely road winds along the rocky russet hills—the epitome of the outback—the Never-Never land. Noble desert trees, dry globes of spinifex, mistletoe, mulga brush; Mount Sonder in the distance resembling a lady reclined on a lofty, elevated rock bed; not a soul around, not one house all along the rusty road; only a few cows trying to cross in front of us.

Dennis' recitation of Paterson's poetry gives it all a sing-song touch:

> Down came a *jumbuck* to drink at the *billabong,*
> Up jumped the *swagman* and grabbed him with glee;
> And he sang as he shoved that jumbuck in his *tucker-bag,*
> "You'll come a-waltzing Matilda with me!"

This is how I'll remember Australia.

7

The Meaning of Life

Saturday, March 4

Margaret and I enjoy our last breakfast together outside on the patio.
Then it's time to go to the airport. The drive takes us down
Larapinta Drive. An overwhelming urge grabs me and I ask
Margaret to stop at the caravan park.

"I'll just be a minute."

"Take your time; we're early," she reassures me.

I walk to the spot one more time—stand quietly, almost reverently. Suddenly the words of my poem demand to be spoken. I
recite them as a kind of farewell, a fitting tribute to Peter, to Alice
and all that happened here.

Alice Springs Revisited

There's a plot of land on Larapinta Drive
in the town of Alice Springs;
it's a few square metres of dusty red sand,
shaded from the heat of the sun.

On that spot a tent was pitched
by a smiling blue-eyed man;

236

it became "home" in more ways than one
as he set up our son's caravan.

He lit the stove, he made the tea
and served it with a twinkling grin
for this was our holiday, this was our time
to indulge in every whim.

We trailed through the town, we climbed Anzac Hill
and he called overseas to those dear.
"Grandpa shaved his beard, I saw kangaroos
and I love you very much, do you hear?"

The lantern glowed soft, we drew our chairs close
and talked far into the night.
Our hearts were at one, we hummed a dear song
and our thirty-year love burned so bright.

He grew very still as he thought of his life,
the years measured out in love.
"It's enough," he said, "What more do I want?
I've been granted beyond and above."

A peace filled his soul that shone forth from his face
as he spoke of freedom to come—
the joy that is ours when we've surrendered all
and can say, "Your will be done."

And so on the morn as the sun arose
in a cloudless clear blue sky,
the filigree leaves became heaven's gate
as a soul soared away with a sigh.

I've returned again to that hallowed place
and wept in the shade of the tree—

and pondered long the sum of his life
the meaning it bears for me.

He loved his Lord and walked in His ways;
he was blessed with prosperity.
His labour bore fruit, his children grew strong
and his grandchildren sat on his knee.

The meaning of life? To walk humbly with God
and trust Him at all of His word;
to love and show mercy, to do what is just—
blessed is that man of the Lord.

Enough. I'm ready to go.

As I board the plane, Margaret waves to me from behind the fence just as she did sixteen months ago. Again, I'm overcome with emotion as we rise into the high blue sky. Again, a kind stewardess asks whether I'd like the three private seats in the back.

I watch Alice grow smaller as we climb. She holds no fear. There's a sense of peace, even joy, despite these copious tears. God came to this little town, and I was privileged to catch a glimpse of glory, to walk with "angels." The time of turmoil and grief was "the time of God's coming to me."

The further I rise, the further Alice recedes.

Thanksgiving

1989

It's October once more; the second year of mourning is almost over. I found it to be true that during the second year we grieve at a different, deeper level. During the first year, every experience was new in the sense that I had not gone that way before. The status of "newly bereaved" brought with it attention and encouragement. On my own during this past year, I've felt so much and often experienced a sinking feeling: this is your life now; this is life lived alone.

We chose a paved path along the Niagara River for our annual Thanksgiving hike last week so that Josh, now battling leukemia and weak with chemo treatments, could ride along in the double stroller with eight-month-old Leah. We chatted and commented how pretty the leaves were, how cold the water looked and "Don't run too far ahead, Kaleb." Our hike was a far cry from the days when Peter boisterously guided us, pointed out a beauty spot, played hide-and-seek behind the trees, and filled the woods with laughter.

But we've adjusted, regrouped, and it was a good day despite all the changes life has thrown our way. I have a deeper understanding of the trite phrase *Life goes on.*

Today at sundown, I return to the river path.

The evening is quiet, as the day has been. I stop to watch a perfectly shaped young tree sparsely decked with golden oval leaves. It seems to have chosen this evening's stillness to release the last of its colourful finery. No wind to tear at the leaves; they just let go and gracefully float to the ground to join the others laid out in a perfect yellow circle beneath. All that beauty–quietly letting go, falling to the earth. Peter said the night before he died, "I've had ten years beyond what I was promised; what more do I want?" He left with laughter on his lips; he let go without a fight, quietly, gracefully.

The golden leaves continue to zigzag down, one by one, glowing disks against an orange sky. A bit of verse comes to mind: "Softly the leaves of memory fall / gently I gather and treasure them all." Two years now, I've plucked memories like leaves from a tree. The joyous colourful ones, the scarred pain-filled ones, each one cried about, laughed about, and laid to rest. I have dreaded the day the tree would be bare. The day I'd say goodbye to my grief; the second death, the final farewell.

Yet now, sitting here beside this brave young tree, I'm beginning to feel I can let go of my sorrow, gently, gracefully, following the example of the leaves.

All that beauty laid to rest. The beauty of a life laid to rest. Grief laid to rest. A lifetime of memories laid to rest.

Yet–not to see decay, as these leaves shortly will. Rather–to live on as a treasured part of who I am.

Epilogue

1994

I climb the church steps hand in hand with Joe. We've just returned from our honeymoon and I feel proud to be walking beside my handsome blue-eyed, grey-haired groom. It's good to hear many say, "Welcome back." (Welcome back from Barbados or welcome back to the couple world?) We take our usual seats. For three years now we've been sitting beside each other in church. We jokingly tell people, "We thought we'd make it legal." Before this the time wasn't right. We were not ready to commit to a permanent relationship.

Singing still stirs deep emotions within me. Today we sing about heaven…

A scene slowly rolls across the front wall of the church. A panorama–a mass of people. Faces are blurred, but one focuses. On the far left is Peter's face, clear light-blue eyes smiling directly at me. I gasp and stare dumbfounded. Further along toward the middle another face focuses and I shift my eyes. I recognize her from Joe's pictures. It's Jenny, his deceased wife. She also looks directly at me, smiles. I hold the fragile scene and hope time will be suspended. Then it blurs with my tears. It fades.

I glance at Joe. He's struggling with emotion. A tear rolls down his cheek. He grasps my hand, squeezes it tightly.

Later in the car I ask, "What touched you so this morning?"

"I saw something." He hesitates, stares across the dashboard. "I saw two faces."

"Really?"

"Yes." He hesitates again. "One was Jenny's, the other was Peter's. They were smiling."

I wait to speak. This is beyond understanding.

Finally I whisper, "I also saw them."

His astonished gaze meets mine. Wordless, we hold the wonderful moment between us. Some feelings just can't be put into language.

Then I venture, "Do you think they were smiling their blessing on our marriage?"

"No doubt—there's not a doubt in my mind—they're blessing us because we've gone on with our lives," Joe answers softly.

Still spellbound, I offer, "It's as if the veil were drawn aside for a moment and we were permitted a glimpse."

Joe nods, holds my eyes and with a tremor whispers, "Yes."

Misty-eyed, he starts the car and slowly winds through quiet streets to our new home.

All shall be well,
And all shall be well,
And all manner of things shall be well (Julian of Norwich).

References

Buechner, Frederick. *Listening to Your Life: Daily Meditations with Frederick Buechner.* Composed by George Connor. San Francisco, CA: HarperSanFrancisco, 1992.

Bloomfield, Harold, Melba Colgrove and Peter McWilliams. *How to Survive the Loss of a Love.* Allen Park, MI: Mary Books/Prelude Press, 2000.

Browning, Elizabeth Barrett. *Elizabeth Barrett Browning: Selected Poems.* New York, NY: St. Martin's Press, 1993, 157.

Cowman, Mrs. Charles E., ed. *Streams in the Desert.* Los Angeles, CA: Cowman Pub., 1955, 27.

de Sainte-Exupéry, Antoine. *The Little Prince.* London, UK: Pan Books Ltd., 1974, 28.

Dickinson, Emily. *Selected poems of Emily Dickinson.* New York, NY: Random House Inc., 1996, XL.

Dixon, Paige. *A Time to Love, A Time to Mourn.* New York, NY: Scholastic Book Services, 1975.

Eliot, T. S. "Little Gidding." In *Four Quartets.* Orlando, FL: Harcourt, Inc., 1943.

Evans, George Essex. "The Women of the West." In *The Collected Verse of G. Essex Evans,* Memorial Edition. Sydney, NSW, AU: Angus and Robertson Ltd., 1928.

Frankl, Viktor. *The Search for Meaning.* New York, NY: Washington Square Press, 1984.

Frost, Robert. "Stopping by Woods on a Snowy Evening." In *Robert Frost's Poems,* 194. New York, NY: Washington Square Press, 1971.

Gibran, Kahlil. *The Prophet.* New York, NY: Alfred A. Knopf, 1988, 29.

Gunn, Mrs. Aeneas. *We of the Never-Never.* Milsons Point, NSW, AU: Random Century Australia Pty Ltd., 1983.

Hurnard, Hannah. *Hinds' Feet on High Places.* London, UK: The Olive Press, 1971.

Hurnard, Hannah. *Way of Healing.* San Francisco, CA: Harper & Row Pub., 1986.

Jackson, Helen Hunt. "September." In *Helen Jackson, Poems,* 206-07. Boston, MA: Roberts Brothers, 1892.

Julian, Dom. "Goodbye, God be with you evening October sky." In *A Severe Mercy,* Sheldon Vanauken, 163. Toronto, ON: Harper & Row, 1977.

Kübler-Ross, Elizabeth. *On Death and Dying.* New York, NY: Simon & Shuster Inc., 1969.

Lewis, C.S. *A Grief Observed.* New York, NY: Harper & Row Pub. Inc., 1977.

Marshall, Catherine. *To Live Again.* New York, NY: McGraw-Hill Book Company Inc., 1957.

Marshall, Catherine and Leonard LeSourd. *My Personal Prayer Diary.* Lincoln, VA: Chosen Books, 1979.

McKenzie, Maisie. *Flynn's Last Camp.* Brisbane, Qld., AU: Boolarong Pub., 1985.

Paterson, Andrew Barton. "The Man from Snowy River." In *Taking the Sun,* 118. Melbourne, Victoria: Longman Cheshire Pty Ltd., 1981.

Paton, Alan. *Instrument of Thy Peace.* New York, NY: The Seabury Press Inc., 1982.

Quoist, Michael. "Prayer." In *The Funeral,* 40. New York, NY: Sheed & Ward imprint of Rowman and Littlefield Publishers, Inc., 1963. Used by permission.

Shute, Nevil. *A Town Like Alice.* London, UK: Pan Books Ltd., 1950.

Smedes, Lewis B. *How Can it be All Right When Everything is All Wrong?* New York, NY: Pocket Books, 1982.

Swindoll, Luci. *Wide My World, Narrow My Bed.* Portland, OR: Multnomah Press, 1982.

Tatelbaum, Judy. *Courage to Grieve.* New York, NY: Harper & Row, 1980.

Tillich, Paul. *The Shaking of the Foundations.* New York, NY: Charles Scribner's Sons, 1955.

Trobisch, Ingrid. *Learning to Walk Alone.* Ann Arbor, MI: Servant Publications, 1985.

Vanauken, Sheldon. *A Severe Mercy.* Toronto, ON: Harper & Row, 1977.

Wiebe, Katie. *Alone: A Search for Joy.* Wheaton, IL: Tyndale, 1976.

Songs

Bennett, Sanford F. "In the Sweet By and By." In *Worship Hymnal.* Hillsboro, KA: Mennonite Brethren Publishing House, 1973.

Boberg, Carl. "How Great Thou Art." Translated by Stuart K. Hine. In *How Great Thou Art Most Famous Hymns.* Wise Publications, 1986.

Elliott, Emily E. S. "Thou Didst Leave Thy Throne." In *The Hymnbook.* New York, NY: Presbyterian Church in the USA, 1955, #184.

Heaver, Rode. "When I Come to the End of the Road." In *Songs for Low Voice.*

Housmann, Julie K. "Take Thou My Hand O Father." Translated by Herman Bruckner. In *Worship Hymnal,* 88. Hillsboro, KA: Mennonite Brethren Pub. House, 1973.

Paterson, Andrew Barton. "Waltzing Matilda." In *Taking the Sun,* 60. Melbourne, Victoria: Longman Cheshire Pty Ltd., 1981.

Wilkin, Maryjohn and Kris Kristofferson. "One Day at a Time Sweet Jesus." Buckhorn Music Publ. Corp., 1973.